*"Katie Orr has both the unique ability to m*
*others and a passion for helping women lo*
*Through her Bible studies, Katie teaches others how to methodically grasp and absorb biblical theology in digestible bite-sized chunks. Her distinct and approachable gift of leading others through Scripture gives those with a desire to dive into God's Word a wonderful opportunity to both understand and apply deep biblical truths in their every day."*

—CHRYSTAL EVANS HURST, coauthor of *Kingdom Woman*

*"Katie Orr is a woman captivated by the Word and person of God. Her heart beats to uncover the truth of Christ for herself and to make those hard-won truths accessible to others. They say that the mark of a good leader is that her work will point people toward God more than herself, and if that's true, then Katie Orr is exactly the kind of leader I personally want to follow."*

—LOGAN WOLFRAM, author of *Curious Faith* and executive director and host of Allume

*"I personally have benefited in countless ways from the FOCUSed15 Bible study method. I am grateful to Katie for her work and for bringing me back to Jesus over and over again in each of these studies.* Everyday Peace *was a safe harbor for me in the middle of life's storms. As with every other book in the series, Katie Orr helps make Bible study easy, helpful, and soul-enriching."*

—JESSICA THOMPSON, author of *Everyday Grace* and coauthor of *Give Them Grace*

*"The Scriptures are like jewels. When you look from different angles they glimmer in beautiful and unexpected ways. The FOCUSed15 Bible study method gives a fresh way to examine and enjoy the most precious words on earth. Katie Orr's zeal for God's Word is contagious and may forever change the way you engage the Bible."*

—JESSE LANE, vice president of connections at Seed Company

*"We all want to spend time studying the Bible and growing our relationship with Jesus. But then life gets busy, and we end up wondering what happened to our good intentions. Katie Orr understands this, and through the FOCUSed15 Bible study method, she's provided a practical and inspirational solution. You'll have the tools you need to do what your heart truly desires."*

—HOLLY GERTH, best-selling author and cofounder of DaySpring's (in)courage blog

*"Katie Orr has designed material for the busy woman in mind—a focused 15 minutes a day that leads the reader to encounter the biblical text with guidance that reinforces solid principles of biblical interpretation and helpful application that makes God's Word come alive in our daily choices."*

—**TREVIN WAX**, Bible and reference publisher for LifeWay Christian Resources

*"Katie Orr has a passion for Scripture and for women to know Scripture. This passion shows in her FOCUSed15 Bible study method, which she uses to lead women through books of the Bible and topical doctrinal studies. She proves that inductive Bible study doesn't have to be complicated but can be deeply impactful and fruitful."*

—**CHRISTINE HOOVER**, author of *From Good to Grace* and *The Church Planting Wife*

*"The FOCUSed15 Bible study method gives women an opportunity to learn the tools of inductive Bible Study in bite-sized chunks. Perfect for anyone who is committed to studying the Word in this time-crunched culture!"*

—**ANDREA BUCZYNSKI**, vice president of global leadership development/human resources for Cru

*"Everywhere I go women are searching for discipleship tools, either for themselves or for those they are discipling. Katie Orr has delivered up a fresh, substantive tool to accomplish both. FOCUSed15 is a serious study method that is possible even for those with demanding responsibilities. This material will fit in a variety of settings and for women everywhere on their spiritual journey."*

—**KATHY FERGUSON LITTON**, national consultant for ministry to pastors' wives, North American Mission Board

*"Katie Orr brings a unique and productive method of studying Scripture to the world of Bible studies. I enthusiastically encourage women to explore this effective and enjoyable method of Bible study!"*

—**SUZIE HAWKINS**, author and longtime member of Southern Baptist Convention Pastors' Wives, wife of O. S. Hawkins

# Other books in the

FOCUSed15 Bible study series

*EVERYDAY* **faith**

*Drawing Near to His Presence*

*EVERYDAY* **hope**

*Holding Fast to His Promise*

*EVERYDAY* **love**

*Bearing Witness to His Purpose*

*EVERYDAY* **peace**

*Standing Firm in His Provision*

# EVERYDAY obedience

Walking Purposefully in His Grace

KATIE ORR

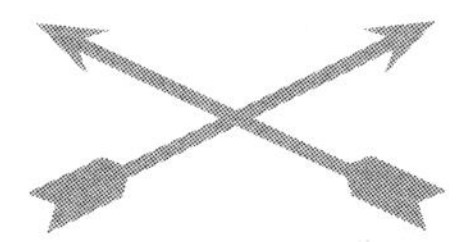

BIRMINGHAM, ALABAMA

New Hope® Publishers
PO Box 12065
Birmingham, AL 35202-2065
NewHopePublishers.com
New Hope Publishers is a division of WMU®.



New Hope Publishers serves its authors as they express their views, which may not express the views of the publisher.

Published in association with the agency of Kirkland Media Management, LLC. of PO Box 1539, Liberty, Texas 77575

Library of Congress Cataloging-in-Publication Data

Names: Orr, Katie, 1978- author.
Title: Everyday obedience : walking purposefully in his grace / Katie Orr.
Description: First [edition]. | Birmingham : New Hope Publishers, 2017.
Identifiers: LCCN 2017004210 | ISBN 9781625915252 (permabind)
Subjects: LCSH: Obedience—Biblical teaching—Textbooks. | Bible. Titus, III—Textbooks.
Classification: LCC BS2755.6.O26 O77 2017 | DDC 234/.6—dc23
LC record available at https://lccn.loc.gov/2017004210



ISBN-13: 978-1-62591-525-2

N174123 • 0417 • 3M1

# Dedication

To my parallel friend, Kristen.

You are a gift to my soul. Your gentleness, wisdom, and grace are a continual light to my own walk of obedience. I'm so thankful God made us friends. Love you.

# Table of Contents

# Introduction

**OBEDIENCE.**

I assume if you hold this study in your hands, you desire to be more obedient. You have sin in your life you want to be rid of. There are parts of your life you don't know how to "give over" fully to God. You want to be a better person. Do more for God. Be more than the average Joe Christian. Yet, the reality of everyday obedience can feel vague and distant, like a mythical creature—heard of but rarely witnessed.

The Christian is called to obedient living. I bet you know this already. In fact, my guess is the amount of do's and don'ts stored up in your mind is enough to stymie even the most faithful of Christians. You want to do right, but there's a big disconnect with the desires of your heart and the reality of your days. Determined, you wake most days with your eyes set toward obedient living. But when the rubber meets the road, you end up in a ditch.

If you're here for another set of directions toward this seemingly illusive obedient life, this Bible study may disappoint. I'm not going to waste your precious time by piling up more commands for you to heed. I have no desire to give you yet another list of rules to follow. Besides, I'm assuming you already have more than you can manage. Throwing more obstacles into our path will not help us toward victory. More rules do not intrinsically lead to more obedience.

Now, you and I certainly have a role to play in our daily pursuit of God. We cannot sit on our rears expecting change to occur or obedient living to simply arrive on our doorstep. There is work to be done. But I've found that we Christians tend to get things backwards. A lot. We try to earn things we were never meant to earn.

Before we go any further, there is something very important that needs to be said. You may or may not have heard this before, and even if you've grown up hearing it, you probably have a hard time believing it's true. Here it is: Jesus has already been perfectly obedient for you. And when you enter into a relationship with Him, His perfect righteousness is gifted to you. Now and forever, God looks on you and sees perfection. Righteousness. Jesus. And because God no longer sees your sin but, instead, His perfect Son's righteousness, God is pleased with you. He is perfectly happy with you. He rejoices over you.

It took me a long time to understand the importance and implications of this truth. Before I heard and truly grasped these truths, I found myself in a familiar trap. Maybe you can relate. After my worst moments, a vision of God would flash through my head: Him standing, arms crossed, face stern, head shaking when He found out about the bad choices I made. Though I knew I was a Christian, I had accepted the lie that I was stuck in the mess of my sin. Alone. Without hope. Forever marked with the burden of failure. The only choices I could see at that point: give up or try harder.

I didn't want to give up because I really, really wanted to please God and be nearer to Him. So, after failing, I jumped back on that hamster wheel and ran even harder. This time, I was determined not to mess things up. Only I did mess things up. Again and again and again.

That try-harder life was exhausting.

Have you been on this try-harder wheel? Maybe you are spinning in it right now, weary from the endless running yet determined to get it right this time. It may even be why you picked up this study. Let me save you from another face-plant: you will not get it right. You can never obey perfectly. Ever. The try-harder life leads to either burnout and frustration or self-dependence and man-made righteousness. Neither of these is what we really want. Neither of these leads to the abundant life Jesus promises.

So if more do's and don'ts are not the key to true and wild obedience, what is? If trying harder to get it right is not the way to go, which direction is?

We need to back up and redefine our understanding of the obedient living to which we are called. Yes, we are called to be holy. Yes, we have decisions to make. Yes, our fellowship and intimacy with God depend on it. However, our motivations for obedience make a big difference.

Obedience is the right response to the grace of God.

Obedience is a heart issue and involves a radical change of direction, purpose, and desire. It is a heart revolution that comes only from outside ourselves; it's only by the provision, power, and presence of Christ that we can ever show an ounce of genuine obedience. With our eyes fixed on grace (instead of our actions), through the power of the Spirit of God, we can fulfill this calling of obedient, godly living. It's not a myth. Everyday obedience can be the reality of your moments.

Over the next four weeks, through Colossians 3:1–17, we'll renew our minds to the realities of who we are because of Christ and how these truths transform our efforts toward obedience. With our efforts rooted in truth and dependent on the grace of God, we'll move forward together into everyday obedience.

Just so you know, I feel wholly inadequate to write this study. My own walk of obedience is as shaky as a toddler learning to walk, though I've been a Christian for 25 years. And after months of deep study and intense writing sessions, I still clumsily stumble through this everyday obedience thing.

I've wanted to start this study from scratch more times than I can count. In fact, I did start it all over once, completely changing the study plan. I've wrestled more with what not to write in this study than what to include. Just about daily I would uncover another truth that would bring a greater understanding, a broader portrait, and a more accurate picture of everyday obedience. And so, I wrestled again and again over what to keep and what to leave out, all the while prayerfully handling the Word and hoping to God I'm not messing this whole thing up.

I had to remind myself that the gospel is like a perfect, stunning, multifaceted diamond. It gleams and reflects beauty at every angle, and every angle invokes a response in us. In *Everyday Obedience*, I'll help you focus on one facet of this diamond. Together we'll move toward rightly responding to all we see through Colossians 3:1–17, just 17 verses pulled out of the whole counsel of Scripture, with only four weeks to study it together.

My point is this: there is oh-so-much more to say about obedience than I can fit into 20 days of study. But, I do believe the Spirit is in this work and, though I am an imperfect messenger, God is faithful to bring the message of the gospel to the hearts of His people. And my hope and prayer is—even through this small peek into the gospel-grace we'll take together over the next four weeks—that you will see our gracious God better and better each day. With the glory due His name, you will learn better how to rightly respond to who He is and how much He loves you. God's grace naturally leads the Christian into obedient worship of Him with our everyday moments.

So, together, let's dive into this study. I'm thrilled you're on this journey with me. Let's go.

# The Need for Focus

**IF THIS IS** your first FOCUSed15 study, you'll want to carefully read through the following introduction and study method instructions. After that, I'll see you on Day 1!

It's hard to focus.

In a world filled with continual demands for my attention, I struggle to keep a train of thought. Tasks I need to do. Appointments I need to remember. Projects I need to complete.

Yeah, it's hard to focus.

Without a good focus for my days, I wander. I lack the ability to choose well and to avoid the tyranny of the urgent. Without focus, days become a blur—tossed back and forth between the pressing and the enticing.

## *Why Focus Matters*

I felt pretty lost during my first attempts at spending time with God in the Bible. After a few weeks of wandering around the Psalms and flipping through the New Testament, I realized I had no clue what I was doing.

It felt like a pretty big waste of time.

I knew the Bible was full of life-changing truths and life-giving promises, but I needed to learn how to focus on the details to see all that Scripture held for me.

In the medical world, we depend on the microscope. Even with all the fancy machines that can give test results in seconds, the microscope has yet to become obsolete. Some things can only be discovered through the lens of the scope.

What looks like nothing to the naked eye is actually teeming with life-threatening bacteria. Even under the microscope, they may not be seen at first glance. But with the smallest adjustment of the focus, the blurry cloud of the field in view is brought into focus and the finest details are revealed.

And those details matter.

You need a microscope to make a diagnosis, but the microscope itself doesn't make the discoveries. It takes a trained eye to distinguish between cells. The average person may be able to figure out how to use the microscope to find a cell and get it in focus, but without training, the beginner will not know the clinical significance of what is seen.

Similarly, when we approach God's Word, we must learn to focus on what we see and develop a trained eye to know its significance.

## *Ready for More*

I grew up in a shallow Christian culture. Don't do drugs. Don't have sex. Don't tell lies. Read your Bible. Be a light—sold-out for Jesus. This was the sum of being a good Christian, or so I thought.

Now, I'm your typical firstborn list-checker, so the do's and don'ts worked for me . . . for a while. But as I got older and the temptations of the don'ts became more enticing, I began to wonder if this Christianity thing was worth it.

Is this really what people spend their lives chasing? Seems tiring—and ultimately worthless.

Yet, God was drawing my heart—I could undeniably feel it—but I knew I was missing something. I thought I'd check out this reading-the-Bible thing. Sure, I had read a devotional or two and knew all the Bible stories, but I didn't feel I knew God Himself.

A bit nervous, I drove to the local bookstore to buy my first really nice Bible. I excitedly drove back home, headed straight to my room, opened up my leather-bound beauty, and began to read . . .

. . . and nothing happened.

I'm not quite sure what I was expecting, but it sure wasn't confusion and frustration. I decided to give it another try the next day and still heard nothing. I had no clue what I was reading.

In all my years of storing up the do's and don'ts in my how-to-be-a-good-Christian box, I never caught a how or why.

For years I stumbled through my black leather Bible with very little learned on the other side of it all. Yet, God was faithful to lead and speak, and I fully believe He can and does speak to us through His Word, even if we are as clueless as I was.

However, I also believe God's Word is meant to be a great catalyst in our growth, and as we pursue how to better know God through His Word, we will experience Him in deeper ways.

You and I need a healthy, rich diet of God's Word in order to grow. And as we read, study, and learn to digest the Bible, we move toward becoming more like Christ. When we pursue the nearness of God, the don'ts become lackluster compared to the life-giving promises of His Word.

## *A FOCUSed 15 Minutes*

Over time, I learned how to use incredible Bible study tools that took my time with God in His Word to a deeper level. Yet with each method, Bible study seemed to take more and more time. Certain seasons of life allow for a leisurely time in the Bible; my experience has proven that most of my days don't.

As much as I would love to find a comfy chair in my favorite local coffee shop and study God's Word for hours, it is just not often possible. I'm lucky if I can get a decent breakfast in every morning before my day starts rolling. Distractions and demands abound, and many days I have not even tried to study my Bible because I just didn't have what it would take, time-wise, to get much out of it.

Until I learned to focus.

Even the busiest Christians can learn to focus and train their eyes to discover the life-changing truths held in Scripture. No incredibly long "quiet times" or seminary degree required.

All it takes is a focused 15 minutes.

The method I will walk you through consists of 15 minutes, five days a week. We will focus on the same set of verses over the course of a week, and each day of that week we will look at the passage with a different lens to gather new insights along the way.

## *Two Ultimate Goals*

My prayer for you as we dive into the Bible is twofold. First, I want to work myself out of a job. I want you to walk away from this study a bit more confident in your ability to focus on the transformational truths of Scripture on your own.

Second, I hope you will encounter our God in a deep and meaningful way through these focused 15 minutes.The most important thing about us is what we believe about God, and my prayer is that you will more accurately understand the truths about who He is through your own study of Scripture. As you get to know our glorious God better and better each day, I think you'll see your actions and attitudes are forever changed—because of who He is.

## *What You'll Need*

A pen to record your study notes and a journal for additional notes and any bonus study work you choose to do.

A Bible. If you don't have one, I recommend investing in a good study Bible. Visit my resources page at KatieOrr.me for solid study Bible suggestions.

Both a Greek interlinear Bible and Greek lexicon. There are in-print and free online versions for both. Check out my resources page for links.

## *A Few Important Notes*

This is only one method. This approach is my attempt at distilling down how I enjoy spending time in God's Word. There are other great methods I use from time to time. Take what you can from this method, and use what works for you. Make it your own.

Fifteen minutes is just the starting point. Some of us are in a stage of life where we'll take 15 minutes whenever we can get it. Others may be able to carve out more time. I will give you suggestions for how to shorten or lengthen the study as needed. I think you will find yourself looking up at the clock and realizing you've accomplished a lot in a short amount of time.

Using online study tools will be of great help. You can certainly do this study without getting online; however, you will expedite many of the processes by utilizing the powerful—and free—online tools I suggest throughout our time together. I totally get that being online while trying to connect with God has its distracting challenges. Do what works for you. There is no "right" way to do this study. The only way to "fail" is to stop meeting with God.

Resist the urge to consult commentaries and study Bible notes right away. I am thankful for all the resources we have at our fingertips, but oftentimes devotionals, study Bibles, and the latest, greatest Bible teacher can be a crutch that keeps us from learning how to walk intimately with God on our own. While I do believe there is only one true meaning of each verse, God has a personalized word to speak to each of us through this study. Receiving big news from a loved one in a deliberate and personalized way means so much more to us than receiving the news third-hand. When the Holy Spirit reveals a message to our hearts through God's Word, it will be something we hold to much more closely than someone else's experience of God. If at the end of the week, you are still unsure of the meaning of the passage, you can then look through commentaries.

For a list of my favorite online and print resources, including Greek study tools, commentaries, cross-referencing tools, and study Bibles, check out my resources page at KatieOrr.me.

# How to FOCUS

**OVER THE NEXT** four weeks, we will study obedience together using the FOCUSed15 study method. Think of me as your Bible coach. I will point you to the goal, give you what you need, and cheer you on—but you'll be the one doing the work.

The FOCUSed15 method may be different from other studies you've completed. We're focusing on quality, not quantity. The goal is not to see how quickly we can get through each verse, but how deeply we can go into each verse and find everything we can about the obedience portrayed. This is how we can go deeper, in as little as 15 minutes a day, by looking at the same passage over the course of several days, each day using a new lens to view it. We're not trying to get everything we can out of the passage the first time we sit in front of it. Instead, we'll come back to it again and again, peeling back each layer, 15 minutes at a time.

Here is where we're headed:

- **Week 1—***What Is Everyday Obedience?*
- **Week 2—***The Foundation of Everyday Obedience*
  *FOCUSing on Colossians 3:1–4*
- **Week 3—***Rightly Responding to Grace: Fight the Flesh*
  *FOCUSing on Colossians 3:5–9*
- **Week 4—***Rightly Responding to Grace: Walk in Holiness*
  *FOCUSing on Colossians 3:10–17*

## *The FOCUSed15 Bible Study Method*

For me, high school history homework typically consisted of answering a set of questions at the end of a chapter. I quickly found that the best use of my time was to take each question, one at a time, and skim through the chapter with the question in mind. So, if the question was about Constantine, I would read the chapter wearing my "Constantine glasses." All I looked for were facts about Constantine.

Little did I know then, this "glasses" method would become my favorite way to study God's Word. The FOCUSed15 method is essentially changing to a new pair of glasses with each read, using a different focus than the read before. Together, we will study one passage for five days, each day using a different part of the FOCUSed15 method.

- **Day 1—***Foundation: Enjoy Every Word*
- **Day 2—***Observation: Look at the Details*
- **Day 3—***Clarification: Uncover the Original Meaning*
- **Day 4—***Utilization: Discover the Connections*
- **Day 5—***Summation: Respond to God's Word*

For each day in our study, I will guide you through a different lens of the FOCUSed15 study method, designed to be completed in as little as 15 minutes a day. There are also bonus study ideas with every day, providing ways to spend more time and dig even deeper if you can. We'll pray together each day, declaring our dependence on the Spirit of God to open the eyes of our hearts to the truths in God's Word.

## *Foundation: Enjoy Every Word*

Many of us are conditioned to read through Scripture quickly and are often left having no idea what we just read. So, to kick off our studies, we will write out our verses. Nothing too fancy, but an incredibly efficient way to slow down and pay attention to each word on the page.

## *Observation: Look at the Details*

With our foundation work behind us, we'll spend this day looking for truths in God's Word. This is a powerful use of our time; we cannot rightly apply the Bible to our lives if we do not accurately see what is there. Observation is simply noting what we see by asking ourselves a set of questions. We're not yet trying to figure out what it means, we are simply beginning an assessment. I will guide you along the way as we look for specific truths like, "What does this passage say is true about obedience?"

## *Clarification: Uncover the Original Meaning*

This is going to be fun. We'll take a peek at the original language of the verses. Our three passages are in the New Testament, so we'll look up the original Greek they were written in. To do this we'll follow three simple steps:

**Step 1: DECIDE which word you would like to study.**

In this step, we will look for any repeated words or keywords, choose one, and learn more about it.

**Step 2: DISCOVER that word as it was originally written.**

Next, using an interlinear Bible, we'll find the original Greek word for the English word we chose in Step 1.

**Step 3: DEFINE that word.**

Finally, we will learn the full meaning of each Greek word using a Greek lexicon, which is very much like a dictionary. We'll walk through an example together each week. You can also bookmark How to Do a Greek Word Study in the appendix for your reference throughout the study.

## *Utilization—Discover the Connections*

*The infallible rule of interpretation of Scripture is the Scripture itself: and therefore, when there is a question about the true and full sense of any Scripture . . . it must be searched and known by other places that speak more clearly.*

—THE WESTMINSTER CONFESSION OF FAITH

Ever notice the little numbers and letters inserted in your study Bible? Most have them. The numbers are footnotes, helpful bits of information about the original text. The little letters are cross-references and important tools for study.

Cross-references do just that, referencing across the Bible where the word or phrase is used in other passages. They may also refer to a historical event or prophecy significant to the verse you are studying.

Together, we will follow a few of the cross-references for each of our passages, as they will often lead us to a better understanding of the main teaching of our verses. If your Bible doesn't have cross-references, no worries! I will provide verses for you to look up and will refer you to online tools for bonus studies.

## *Summation–Respond to God's Word*

*A respectable acquaintance with the opinions of the giants of the past, might have saved many an erratic thinker from wild interpretations and outrageous inferences.*

—CHARLES SPURGEON

This is when we begin to answer the question, "How should this passage affect me?" To understand this we will take three actions:

1. **Identify—Find the main idea of the passage.**

   With a robust study of our passage accomplished, we can now do the work of interpretation. Interpretation is simply figuring out what it all means. This is oftentimes difficult to do. However, if we keep in mind the context and make good observations of the text, a solid interpretation will typically result.

   This is when we will finally consult our study Bibles and commentaries! Commentaries are invaluable tools when interpreting Scripture. They are available on the entire Bible, as well as volumes on just one book of the Bible. For a list of free online commentaries, as well as in-print investments, check out KatieOrr.me/Resources.

**2. Modify—Evaluate my beliefs in light of the main idea.**

Once we have figured out what the passage means, we can now apply the passage to our lives. Many tend to look at application as simply finding something to change in their actions. Much in the Bible will certainly lead us to lifestyle changes, but there is another category of application that we often miss: what we believe.

We must learn to see the character of God in what we study and ask ourselves how our view of Him lines up with what we see. Of course it is helpful to look for do's and don'ts to follow, but without an ever-growing knowledge of who God is, the commands become burdensome.

**3. Glorify—Align my life to reflect the truth of God's Word.**

When we see God for the glorious, grace-filled Savior He is, the natural response is worship; the do's and don'ts become a joy as they become a way to honor the One we love with our lives. Worship is true application.

## *All of This . . . in 15 Minutes?*

Yes, I know this seems like a lot of ground to cover. Don't worry! I will be here to walk you through each day. Remember, instead of trying to go as fast as we can through a passage, we are going to take it slowly and intentionally. We'll look at one passage for an entire week, and apply one part of the method to the passage each day.

## *The Cheat Sheet*

At the end of most days' studies, I've included a "cheat sheet." While trying to complete a Bible study, I've often been paralyzed with wondering, *Am I doing this the right way?* The cheat sheet is there for you to use as a reference point. It is not a list of correct answers, however, and is meant instead to provide just a little bit of guidance here and there to let you know you are on the right track.

There are also several references in the appendix you may want to consult throughout our time together. If you are new to Bible study, you might consider spending a day to read through the appendices before beginning your study. I hope those pages will be a great help to you.

## *A Note to the Overwhelmed*

Bible study is not a competition or something to achieve. It is a way of communicating with our magnificent God. If you have little time or mental capacity (I've been there, moms with little ones!), ignore the bonus study ideas and enjoy what you can. Keep moving through the study each day, and know that you have taken a step of obedience to meet with God in His Word. Other seasons of life will allow for longer, deeper study. For now, embrace these precious moments in the Word, and remember that Jesus is your righteousness. When God looks at you—overwhelmed and burned-out though you are—He sees the faithful obedience and perfection of Christ on your behalf, and He is pleased. Rest in that today, weary one.

# WHAT IS Everyday Obedience?

# Obedience: The Right Response to the Grace of God

*But if it is by grace, it is no longer on the basis of works; otherwise grace would no longer be grace. —Romans 11:6*

**SIR LANCELOT, A** young French prince, grew up with a dream of moving to Camelot, in England. According to tales of old, Lancelot, in hopes of proving himself worthy of becoming one of the Knights of the Round Table, departed France to find King Arthur of England and show what a great knight he was.

Once in England, he encountered a group of knights. Assuming them to be the bad guys, he fought them with fervor. One by one, Sir Lancelot singlehandedly disarmed each attacking knight. After the onslaught, he found himself surrounded by people who were cheering and congratulating him for his victories. Foremost among the people was a king. Sir Lancelot had stumbled into this king's tournament, and the king was very impressed with the young, skillful, foreign knight. He offered him a seat at his royal court of knights on the spot. Lancelot, eager to move on from this detour and back on to his pursuit of King Arthur and the Knights of the Round Table, answered the king's questions politely and then respectfully declined this unknown king's offer of knighthood.

Little did he know, the tournament he had victoriously dominated was actually King Arthur's. The very king he was looking for had been found. The glorious first impression Lancelot longed to make had been made. This king's offer for a seat at the table was the very one he'd longed for.

Once Lancelot realized he was in the presence of King Arthur, he was immediately humbled and distraught. For sure, he thought, he had messed up his one chance to make a good first impression. His armor was dirty, his hair disheveled, his best foot not forward. Yet, what he didn't realize was that he'd already been accepted by King Arthur before he had spoken one word.

We too have been accepted by the King into His imperial household. But unlike Sir Lancelot, our acceptance is not because of our grand performance. We've been given royal status and all that accompanies the life of a noble, through the performance and sacrifice of Jesus. He lived a life of perfection, died a death of redemption, and rose from the dead to bring power over corruption.

Though we try to make it a whole lot more complicated than this, obedience is simply the right response to God's grace. But often we respond to God's invitation into daily fellowship and abundant living like Sir Lancelot: thanks, but I still have a ton of work to do in order to please the king. We think we have to try harder and harder to earn God's approval. We believe the lie that we have to clean ourselves up and make sure all our ducks are in a row before we can come to God. The battle has been fought and won, and we have already been invited to sit with and enjoy the presence of the King because, "by the one man's obedience the many will be made righteous" *(Romans 5:19).*

1. Take a moment to begin your study in prayer. Use the space provided to journal a prayer, asking the Spirit of God to open your eyes to what the Bible has to say about obedience. Thank

God for His gift of grace. Commit to follow as He leads over these next four weeks of study.

I'm excited for the journey we have ahead of us. Before we get to this verse-by-verse study, we need to take a look at the biblical definition of obedience. During this first week of study, we're going to look through various passages to get a clearer picture of what obedience is—and what it is not. Obedience is not a list of rules to follow. It is not meant to keep us in line or keep us from having fun. Obedience is our purpose as a child of God. It's a daily dance of celebration, a continual act of worship.

We'll start by looking at the truths of the gospel—the good news about all Christ has done for us to bring us into relationship with him. To truly understand the beauty and gravity of all we have through Christ, we need to understand the depth and ugliness of our depravity.

2. Look up Titus 3:3–7. In the cross diagram on page 37, jot down all you learn about mankind to the left of the cross under "Before Christ."

**Before Christ**

*The Work of Christ*

**After Christ**

*By Grace through Faith*

Lest we begin to think, *I'm not that bad!* Romans 3:23 reminds us that "all have sinned and fall short of the glory of God." We can always find someone to compare ourselves to—someone we think we are better than—but the spiritual standard by which we are measured is not people to our right or left. We are measured by

the perfection of our holy God. Anything less than that perfect righteousness is not enough. Our sin-stained world has been permanently and thoroughly pierced by sin. From the first fall of Adam *(Genesis 3)*, we have all inherited a sin nature that invades every part of our being *(Romans 5:12)*. And this nature separates us from God, but God's love has overcome this curse, and Christ's obedience has made a way for us to return to a right, eternal relationship with God.

3. Now read Titus 3:3–7 again, looking for truths to fill in the right side of the cross on page 37 with all we have through the sacrifice of Christ, the free gift of God.

"For the wages of sin is death, but the free gift of God is eternal life in Christ Jesus our Lord" *(Romans 6:23)*. Though I have heard these truths about the free gift of salvation over and over again, it's in my nature to work for it. Something inside drives me to prove myself worthy of this gift. Instead of accepting and embracing mercy and grace with eagerness, I turn my back on it and attempt to build my own bridge to God. Where there should be rest and worship, I choose work and self-reliance. This is not obedience.

4. To close our study today, take a peek at Romans 4:4–5 and 4:16, and write what you learn for each type of person.

| The One Who Works | The One Who Does Not Work But Believes |
|---|---|
| Wages are debt not grace | Justification through Jesus Righteousness |

Early on in my Christian walk, I lived a life much like Lancelot. I didn't realize the King had already invited me into His fellowship—I had already been accepted. I was fully loved. There was no need to keep fighting for His approval. I knew Jesus had died for my sins to forgive me—I had been given mercy—and I was brought into a righteous standing with God. But, I thought from there I had to keep going, keep proving myself worthy, keep trying to get God to be pleased with me. What I didn't understand then (and what I often forget now) is I have not only been shown mercy—God has lavished on me heaps of grace.

It's important to understand the difference between mercy and grace. To show mercy is to withhold punishment. If I'm caught speeding, and the police officer lets me off with a verbal warning, that's mercy. He didn't give me what I deserve. But if the same police officer pulls me over for a speeding violation, gives me a verbal warning along with a trillion dollars, the keys to a new oceanfront mansion, and a lifetime supply of Starbucks coffee, well, that's a whole lot more than mercy. That's grace. That's giving me gifts I do not deserve.

So, when I attempt to save myself, I strip away all that is beautiful from God's great act of grace in my life. I keep trying to earn enough to pay rent on an apartment, disregarding the oceanfront mansion that my Father has already given me.

Though my actions will never be enough, God's act of mercy—Jesus' death on the Cross—is sufficient to cover my debt. God's gift of grace—Jesus' sinless life and powerful Resurrection—is my continual sustenance and constant foundation from which I am able to be in relationship with a holy God. "That is why it depends on faith, in order that the promise may rest on grace" *(Romans 4:16)*. When

I grasp these glorious gospel realities, I am overwhelmed with gratitude and worship. And from this place, I obey. I am not saved by my obedience. I am saved, and I get to respond to the mercy and grace of God by one great act of worship: obedience. This is my purpose.

> *For by grace you have been saved through faith. And this is not your own doing; it is the gift of God, not a result of works, so that no one may boast. For we are his workmanship, created in Christ Jesus for good works, which God prepared beforehand, that we should walk in them. —Ephesians 2:8–10*

*{God, I am overwhelmed by Your grace for me. I do not deserve it. I never will. Just as His great love for You fueled Christ to become obedient to the point of death on a Cross, may the same love compel me toward a life of holiness. By the power of Your Spirit, I long to live a life of worshipful obedience.}*

## *Bonus Study*

Look up the background, purpose, and audience of Colossians. Most study Bibles will include this information at the beginning of each book. Check the resources page at KatieOrr.me for study Bible suggestions, as well as free online tools you can use.

# Cheat Sheet

2. Look up Titus 3:3–7. In the cross diagram below, jot down all you learn about mankind to the left of the cross under "Before Christ."

3. Now read Titus 3:3–7 again, looking for truths to fill in the right side of the cross below with all we have through the sacrifice of Christ, the free gift of God.

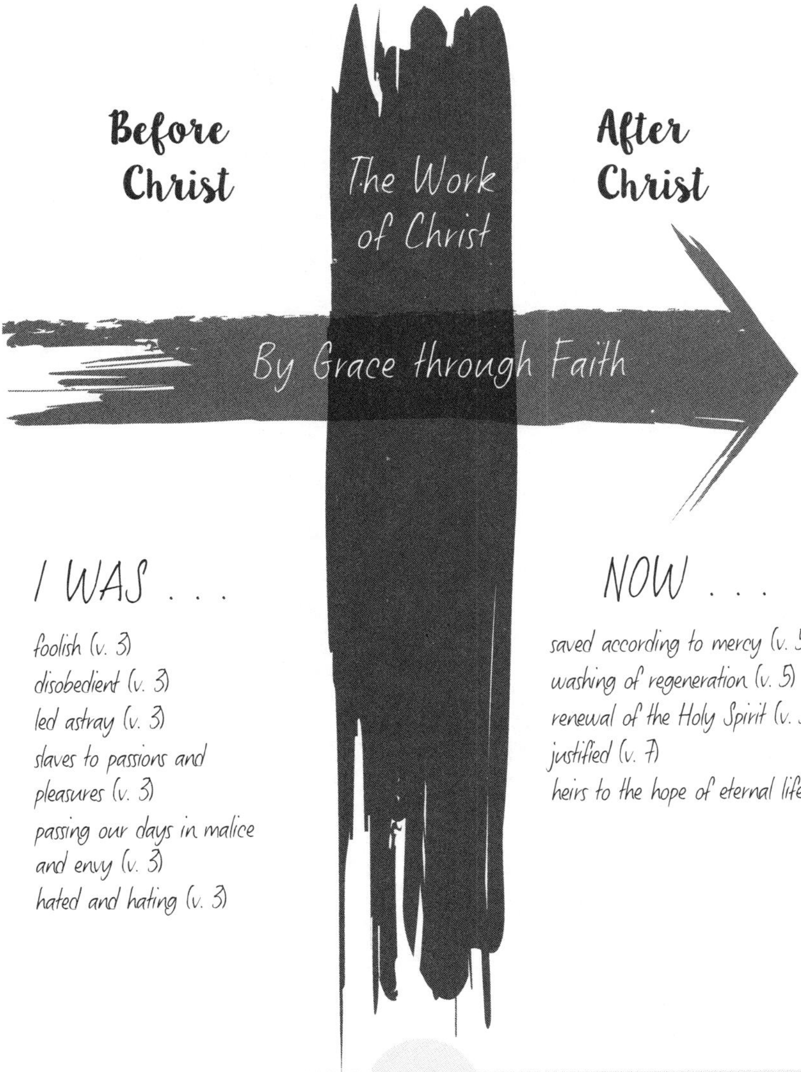

**Before Christ**

**The Work of Christ**

**After Christ**

By Grace through Faith

I WAS . . .

*foolish (v. 3)*
*disobedient (v. 3)*
*led astray (v. 3)*
*slaves to passions and pleasures (v. 3)*
*passing our days in malice and envy (v. 3)*
*hated and hating (v. 3)*

NOW . . .

*saved according to mercy (v. 5)*
*washing of regeneration (v. 5)*
*renewal of the Holy Spirit (v. 5)*
*justified (v. 7)*
*heirs to the hope of eternal life (v. 7)*

4. To close our study today, take a peek at Romans 4:4–5 and 4:16, and write what you learn for each type of person.

| The One Who Works | The One Who Does Not Work But Believes |
| --- | --- |
| His wages are not counted as a gift but as his due. | His faith is counted as righteousness. |

# Obedience: Enabled by the Holy Spirit

*Or do you not know that your body is a temple of the Holy Spirit within you, whom you have from God? You are not your own, for you were bought with a price. So glorify God in your body. —1 Corinthians 6:19–20*

**MY KIDS LOVE** to make chocolate milk. When they first pour the chocolate syrup in the milk, the glass reveals the "chocolate" milk: a glass full of white and a big blob of brown on the bottom. Technically, they've made milk with chocolate in it. But they often forget the last step of chocolate milk-making: stir it up! Once they insert the spoon into the cup and stir the chocolate up into the milk, they finally get a homogenous yummy brown glass of chocolate milk. Oftentimes, they pour themselves too much and are unable to finish the glass of milk right away, so they place it in the fridge to keep for later. When they return to it the chocolate has settled. Technically speaking, it's still chocolate milk, but it no longer looks like it. The effects of the chocolate sauce are no longer evident. They have to stir it back up if they want every sip to be sweet again.

When I first came to Christ in seventh grade, many things changed for me. Once in darkness—sin-stained, lost, and without hope—I was granted new spiritual life, a new nature, right standing before God, and many great and precious promises. Though my eternal landscape changed irrevocably, my immediate lifestyle and patterns did not. Like the glass of milk, I was forever changed into something new and better. The Holy Spirit was permanently

poured into my life and dwells with me every moment of every day. But just like the chocolate in my glass, He will not fill every ounce of my life if not continually stirred. Some moments, He saturates my every thought, emotion, and action. Other times, I deny His transforming presence to reign and rule, and my life looks just like my old "white milk" days without Christ. Instead of being a beacon of God's glory and fame to those around me through my attitude and actions, His presence in my life becomes unnoticeable.

Moment-by-moment obedience is the part we play in the chocolate milk-making of our everyday lives. It picks up a spoon and stirs, inviting God to permeate every part of our days, leading to an incredible filling of His presence. Because we are filled with this presence, when others encounter us, they see the "chocolate" in us, the undeniable presence and character of God.

With every choice, every moment of our day, we either allow God's Spirit to fill every part of our being, or we stuff Him down to the bottom of our glass. Just as the glass with the chocolate syrup sitting on the bottom doesn't look much different from the glass without any chocolate, Christians with the Spirit stuffed down into the bottom of their lives don't look much different from those who are without the Spirit.

Obedience is hard. And everyday, moment-by-moment obedience? Well, that just seems impossible sometimes. When I remember that it's not solely up to me to obey, but that I have been invited to walk hand in hand with the Spirit of God, I can allow Him free reign into every part of my life—that's something only the power of God can achieve. The Spirit is meant to fill our every word, action, thought, and feeling. He is our comforter, counselor, advocate, and help for everyday living. And as He fills every part of our glass, He enables us even more toward obedient living.

In the weeks to come we are going to look at three ways we are to respond to God's grace and walk forward in obedience. But before we get there, we must understand the needed undercurrent for our every action: the power of the Holy Spirit. Without the empowering presence of God's Spirit in our lives, any effort we make will bring us back to our insufficient self-righteousness. That, and complete exhaustion. "And God is able to make all grace abound to you, so that having all sufficiency in all things at all times, you may abound in every good work" *(2 Corinthians 9:8)*.

1. Declare your utter need for the Spirit of God to change your heart and your ways. Invite Him to rise up and fill every part of your life.

2. Look up the following verses, and note what you learn to be true about the Holy Spirit.

John 14:17 – Holy Spirit dwells in me

John 14:26 – Holy Spirit teaches us and helps us remember Gods words.

Romans 8:26–27

I cannot obey without His enabling power. This power ultimately comes from God, through the presence of His Spirit in my life.

3. Look up 2 Peter 1:3. What does this verse say the power of God grants us? He gives us all things that pertain to life + godliness

I love the way the *New Living Translation* puts this truth: "By his divine power, God has given us everything we need for living a godly life." Everything we need. By His divine power. Obedience is not out of reach if we are relying on the power of God. Not only is it now within our grasp but it is also an expected fruit of those who are in Christ. If the Spirit of God is within us, we will obey. This does not mean we will obey perfectly, but it does mean there is always part of us that longs for a more obedient life.

Though we may understand we enter into a relationship by God's grace through faith alone (not works), wholly dependent on the power of God to save us, we often move from salvation into "I got this" mode and leave behind our need for God. As the Apostle Paul says, "How foolish can you be? After starting your new lives in the Spirit, why are you now trying to become perfect by your own human effort?" *(Galatians 3:3 NLT)*. We need the power of God today just as much as we did the first moment we depended on it for salvation.

*{God, help me to see where I am attempting to live my life on my own strength. I am desperate for your grace to be an enabling power for the everyday change I so long to experience. Help me make my moments a continual concert of your praise.}*

## *Bonus Study*

Continue your study of the Holy Spirit with these additional verses.

1 Corinthians 2:10

1 Corinthians 6:19

Read through Colossians 2, searching for more truths about your life before and after Christ, and add them to your cross diagram from yesterday's study (p. 37).

Continue to look for and record all the truths about Jesus in Colossians 2.

# Cheat Sheet

2. Look up the following verses, and note what you learn to be true about the Holy Spirit.

John 14:17

*the Spirit of truth*
*the world cannot receive Him*
*the world neither sees Him nor knows Him*
*believers know Him*
*dwells with me*
*will be in me*

John 14:26

*Helper*
*sent by the Father*
*will teach me all things*
*will bring to me remembrance the words of Christ*

Romans 8:26–27

*helps me in my weakness*
*intercedes for me in prayer, according to the will of God*

3. What does 2 Peter 1:3 say this power grants us?

*"All things that pertain to life and godliness, through the knowledge of him who called us to his own glory and excellence."*

# *Bonus Study*

Continue your study of the Holy Spirit with these additional verses.

1 Corinthians 2:10

God reveals truth to me through the Spirit
searches everything, even the depths of God

1 Corinthians 6:19

lives within me
sent from God

# Obedience: A Call to Worship

*In the same way, let your light shine before others, so that they may see your good works and give glory to your Father who is in heaven. —Matthew 5:16*

**ONCE UPON A** time, I thought I was called to the medical field. At first, I entertained thoughts of becoming a doctor, but then decided I didn't want to be in school forever. Instead, I chose the degree medical technology, mainly because the class list sounded like a ton of fun. Beyond the typical biology and physiology courses, I got to dive into advanced hematology, analytical and organic chemistry, and parasitology. (I'm such a nerd.) But when it came time to prepare an exit strategy from college, spending my days in the lab didn't appeal to me. I even looked into medical missions work. But, I knew I was called to something different; I was just beginning to see that God built me to teach, train, and encourage women. I'm grateful for my major, and I really did love all the classes. But as I drew nearer and nearer to graduation, it became more and more apparent God was not calling me to the medical field.

I have friends who light up when they get to talk about math concepts. Others find joy in preparing crafts and lessons for children. Some love to keep paperwork in order. Several friends get to help bring babies into the world. We each receive passions and callings that typically lead to our vocations in life. You might teach math full-time to third graders, work as a nurse in the intensive care unit, keep numbers straight at a bank, stay home to help watch your grandkids, or homeschool and homestead. The specific callings each of us have are varied and vast in number. I like to call them "little c" callings. They are each important and needed and good, and beyond vocation, we have callings that are tied up in our relationships. Sister. Wife. Child. Co-worker. Neighbor. Mother. Friend.

We all have "Big C" callings as well. One such calling is obedience to God. The call to a lifestyle of holiness and God-centered moments is all over Scripture. It's easy to fall into the trap of thinking we are too busy, life is too difficult, or God doesn't understand the struggles we face, which makes it hard for us to walk in holiness in every situation. But the Bible is clear that we can and must live a life of obedience. Though our salvation is certain, there is still much at stake in how we live out our moments.

> *For the love of Christ controls us, because we have concluded this: that one has died for all, therefore all have died; and he died for all, that those who live might no longer live for themselves but for him who for their sake died and was raised. —2 Corinthians 5:14–15*

1. Open today's time in the Word with a short prayer asking God to open your eyes to the truths in this passage.

2. Read Romans 1:1–5. This is a letter written by the Apostle Paul to the church in Rome. Note what you learn from verse 1 about how Paul views himself. Servant of Jesus

3. Now take another look at Romans 1:5, and this time look for the purpose Paul gives for the "grace and apostleship" he had been given. Obedience to the faith.

4. Lastly, look one more time at Romans 1:5. For what sake does Paul say the "obedience of faith" is ultimately for?

   For Jesus' name Sake

Paul's specific, "little c" calling was as an apostle, a temporary position used mightily by God. Paul's "little c" calling was laser-focused and tailor-made for his specific background and God-given strengths. Yet he states he was "set apart for the gospel of God." You and I are too. We all have different callings, individualized for God's unique purpose for our lives. Yet we all have the same overarching "Big C" calling: we are "set apart for the gospel of God" in the specific spaces in which we dwell.

Like Paul, we must view ourselves as instruments of God. Our salvation and unique gifts and callings are to be used for the glory of God. Every step we take needs to be in view of that purpose. We've received great mercy and grace, and it is not meant to stop with us. We remain on this earth for a purpose: to walk, by this gifted grace, a life of obedient worship for the sake of God's glory—spreading His fame into all the world.

» *I appeal to you therefore, brothers, by the mercies of God, to present your bodies as a living sacrifice, holy and acceptable to God, which is your spiritual worship. Do not be conformed to this world, but be transformed by the renewal of your mind, that by testing you may discern what is the will of God, what is good and acceptable and perfect.* —Romans 12:1–2 «

True obedience is God-centered. We obey not to prove ourselves worthy, or out of anything we owe God. Obedience is not meant to have people say, "Wow! Look at you!" Obedience is meant to point others to Christ. Obedience says. "Wow! Look at Him!"

Obedience is worship.

*{God, show me where I've made obedience all about me. Reveal the places in which I have made my "little c" callings more important than the calling to be set apart for the gospel. I am so thankful You saved me. Use me as a vessel to bring others into a relationship with You.}*

## *Bonus Study*

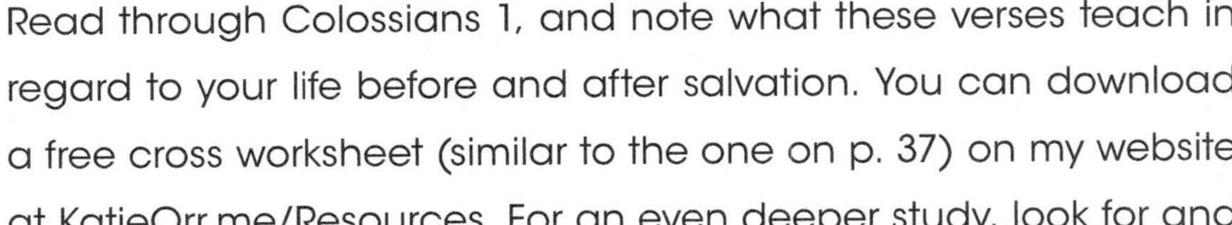

Read through Colossians 1, and note what these verses teach in regard to your life before and after salvation. You can download a free cross worksheet (similar to the one on p. 37) on my website at KatieOrr.me/Resources. For an even deeper study, look for and record all the truths Colossians 1 teaches about Jesus.

# Cheat Sheet

2. Read Romans 1:1–5. Note what you learn from verse 1 about how Paul views himself.

   *servant of Christ*
   *called to be an apostle*
   *set apart for the gospel of God*

3. Now take another look at Romans 1:5, and this time look for the purpose Paul gives for the "grace and apostleship" he had been given.

   *to bring about the obedience of faith for the sake of his name among all the nations*

4. Lastly, look one more time at Romans 1:5. For what sake does Paul say "the obedience of faith" is ultimately for?

   *God's name among all the nations*

# Obedience: A Work of Grace

> *And I am sure of this, that he who began a good work in you will bring it to completion at the day of Jesus Christ. —Philippians 1:6*

**CONTRARY TO POPULAR** belief, Christianity is not about the do's and don'ts. It's not about behavior management. It's not about being better than everyone else. We don't work our way to heaven. Though our salvation is not dependent on our good deeds, our actions do matter. If they didn't, the Bible wouldn't be filled with commands. Train, abide, put on, put off, do this, don't do that. Obedience involves all these commands, and more, but we need to be careful to get the order straight in our hearts and minds.

Today, let's cut to the chase and dive in. We have a lot to cover.

1. Pray for focus. Ask God to help you see the thread of grace needed in our obedience today.

2. Open your Bible to Philippians 2:12–13. Let's start first with what is true about God. What actions does He take?

God works in me to will + work for His good pleasure.

Submit - to order Under
Choosing

The NLT translates verse 13, "For God is working in you, giving you the desire and the power to do what pleases him." God is at work to bring about obedience in us. In Day 2, we looked at how He gives us the power to walk in obedience, but here we learn He also gives us the desire to do what pleases Him. With this nugget of truth, let's go back to Philippians 2.

3. Read Philippians 2:12–13 again. This time, list out the commands given in verse 12.

(1) obey as you always have
(2) not just in my presence but in my absence as well.
(3) work out your own salvation w/ fear & trembling

Paul defines obedience here as working out our salvation. The Greek word for "work out" is also translated "bring about" or "produce." Like a garden we've inherited, we work out that which has already been planted. This same word is used in Romans 15:18.

4. Look up Romans 15:17–18, and record all you learn about Paul's work for God.

I have a reason to be proud of my work for God

Its what Jesus accomplishe through him.

5. Now, read 1 Corinthians 15:10, another letter written by Paul, and note what he says about himself.

I am what I am because of the Grace of God
His grace toward me is not in vain
Its not me but the grace of God

6. To what did Paul attribute his hard work?

7. One more passage. Look up Titus 2:11–14, and note what is true about the grace of God.

God's grace rescued me, and God's grace continues to carry me. God's grace brought salvation and God's grace trains me to work out that salvation. I have work to do. I have choices to make. But the undercurrent of it all is God's grace. Grace is my dancing partner. It leads me out onto the stage to dance a holy dance for my Father. The cool thing is, though I dance for an audience of One, to the glory of Him alone (not me), the world is watching. My grace-enabled performance displays the work of God through me, and by His grace many more can join the dance of grace themselves. "For from him and through him and to him are all things. To him be glory forever. Amen" *(Romans 11:36)*.

*{God, help me to understand this dance of grace. Help me to keep the order straight. Enable me to keep in step with Your Spirit. I'm grateful I don't have to earn Your approval by my performance. Let my performance be a testimony to Your grace.}*

## *Bonus Study*

Read Colossians 3. We'll dig deep into Colossians 3:1–17 together, beginning next week. For now, note the commands given in Colossians 3:18–25.

# Cheat Sheet

2. Open your Bible to Philippians 2:12–13. Let's start first with what is true about God. What actions does He take?

   *God who works in me*
   *to will and*
   *to work*
   *for His good pleasure*

3. Read Philippians 2:12–13 again. This time, list out the commands given in verse 12.

   *obey as you have always obeyed*
   *not just in My presence but also in My absence*
   *work out your own salvation with fear and trembling*

4. Look up Romans 15:17–18, and record all you learn about Paul's work for God.

   *I have reason to be proud of my work for God,*
   *in Christ Jesus*
   *it is what Christ accomplished through him*

5. Now, read 1 Corinthians 15:10, another letter written by Paul, and note what he says about himself.

   *but by the grace of God I am what I am*
   *His grace toward me was not in vain*
   *I worked harder than any*
   *though it was not I but the grace of God*
   *that is with me*

6. To what did Paul attribute his hard work?

the grace of God that is with me

7. Look up Titus 2:11–14, and note what is true about the grace of God.

the grace of God appeared
bringing salvation for all people
training us to renounce ungodliness and worldly passions
to live self-controlled, upright, and godly lives in the present age
waiting for our blessed hope: the appearing of the glory of Jesus

# Obedience: Responding to God's Grace

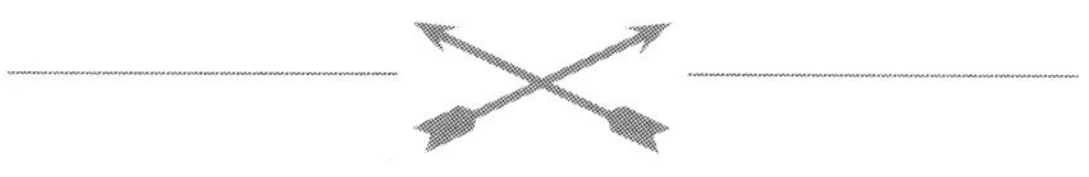

*If you love me, you will keep my commandments. –John 14:15*

**MY WORKS CANNOT** save me. God's mercy saved me.

Jesus took on my sin and paid the debt it demanded, through His death on the Cross and subsequent Resurrection, and when I turned to Him in faith as my Savior, my slate was wiped clean. Yet there was even more that occurred in this glorious moment: Christ gave me His righteousness. The perfect life He lived on this temptation-filled world was credited to me. And now, when God sees me, He sees the perfect life of Christ. His acceptance of me depends solely on the perfect obedience of Jesus. And now I get to live a life in continual response to His mercy.

Obedience is not a reluctant duty. Obedience is not an indebted action. Nor is it the way to salvation. Obedience is a response to God's grace—the natural and right response to this great gift of grace we've received.

1. Take a moment to look back on your studies so far. Pause and ask the Holy Spirit to speak to your heart today as you reflect on all you've learned this week.

Let's take some time to slow down and digest what we've been learning. This is when we begin to answer the question, "How should what I've learned affect me?" As we move toward application, journal through the following questions.

2. Do I tend to obey out of a response to God's grace or an attempt to receive acceptance from Him?

3. When I think of God looking at me, what words tend to define the picture in my mind's eye? (Circle the words that come closest to how you feel God sees you when you are at your worst.)

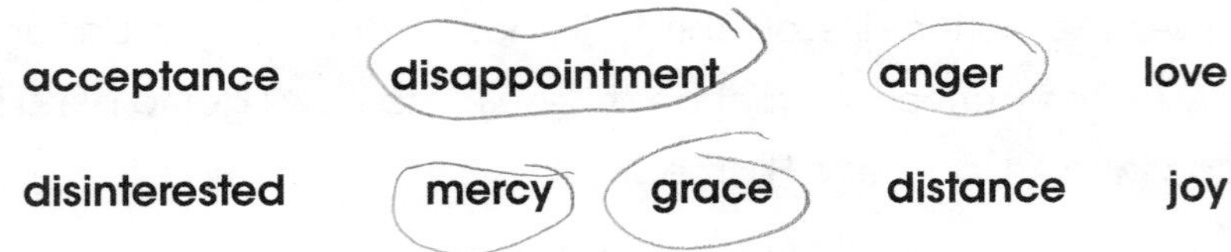


4. How do these words line up with what God says is true about my position before Him?

5. What are some of my "little c" callings? How can I better fulfill my "Big C" calling to be set apart for the gospel as I carry out my everyday living?

6. Which passage from yesterday's study helps me understand better the role I play alongside of God's grace working in me? How can I carry this verse close to me today?

All too often, I get the cart before the horse. I default to self-effort and control. I act as if I still need saving, or I attempt to prove myself worthy of being chosen by God. But I am already chosen, already saved. The work has been done. My debt has been paid. Therefore, I obey.

It is essential that we get this order straight. Because I have been saved, I obey. Because I have been given new life, I obey. Because I have entered into a relationship with the God of the universe, I obey. "If you love me, you will keep my commandments" *(John 14:15)*.

Obedience is responding to His love, grace, and mercy with worship through my everyday moments. Because, though our relationship with our Holy God is not dependent on our actions, our intimacy with Him is. Like a refrigerator that is not working properly, if we fail to work out our purpose through obedient, worshipful living, it will lead to decay. Though obedience is difficult and requires great effort and diligence, it is a partnership. A beautiful dance where we sway with the Spirit of God, resulting in the abundant life promised us in Scripture.

*{God, I get all this backward so often! I am thankful for Your faithful, gentle whispers of correction. Continue to show me where I am depending solely on my own efforts instead of in tandem with the work of Christ on the Cross provided to me.}*

## *Bonus Study*

Read Colossians 4. Add to your list of commands from yesterday's bonus study.

# THE FOUNDATION OF Everyday Obedience

FOCUSING ON
**COLOSSIANS 3:1–4**

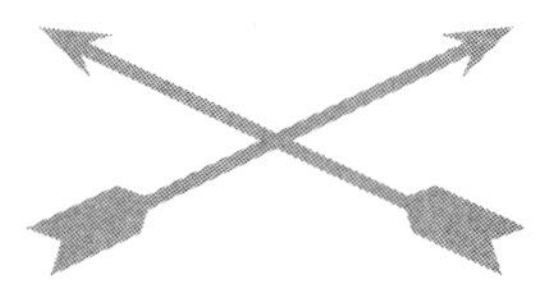

# Foundation

## FOCUSing on Colossians 3:1–4

*But if it is by grace, it is no longer on the basis of works; otherwise grace would no longer be grace. —Romans 11:6*

*Jesus loves me this I know, for the Bible tells me so.*

—ANNA BARTLETT WARNER, 1859

**THE SUMMER SUN** cast its warmth on my shoulders as I enjoyed the Myrtle Beach sand between my toes. Flip-flops dangling from my hand, I walked alongside ladies seasoned in this faith-walk and listened intently to their timely advice. About to begin my senior year in college—on the brink of decisions that would affect my quickly approaching future—I soaked in their words of wisdom. One truth lingers in my heart and mind to this day: the most important beliefs I hold are those I believe about God and about myself.

The Apostle Paul understood this. In fact, after becoming a Christian, Paul poured out his life to preach the truth of who God is and how we—desperate sinners—can enter into a relationship with God and pursue intimate fellowship with Him in our everyday moments. Paul traveled far and wide to bring this good news to every soul who would listen, and congregations of new believers were birthed in the wake of his journey. He often penned truth-filled letters of encouragement, correction, and exhortation to these new churches. Much of the New Testament is made up of these letters, one of which is the Book (or letter, really) of Colossians.

Over the next three weeks, we are going to dive into a portion of this letter, Colossians 3:1–17. Paul was prompted to write to the church at Colossae when he received reports of a dangerous false doctrine being preached among the new believers. And so, because he understood that what we believe influences our actions and attitudes, he was driven to send truth to combat the lies they were hearing and beginning to believe.

1. Before we dive into Colossians 3, spend a moment in prayer. Ask God to open your eyes to the life-changing truths in this passage.

Now it's time to start using the FOCUSed15 study method. We'll study the same passage all week, giving us a chance to pull back and look at these verses through different lenses each day.

## *Enjoy Every Word*

2. We'll work through our first layer of studying Colossians 3:1–4 by copying the passage. This is designed to help us slow down and begin to grasp what is going on in the passage. Reading with intentionality creates a slowness that allows for better understanding. You can write out the verses word-for-word, diagram them, or draw pictures or symbols to help you begin to understand what is being said. There is no right or wrong way

to do this. It is simply an exercise of intentionally to take in each word. We'll build on what we learn from this practice throughout the rest of the week.

3. Record any questions you have about this passage. Your questions should be answered by the end of the week, as you continue to study. If not, you'll have an opportunity to consult commentaries later.

4. To close our time today, take a quick peek at Colossians 1:9–10. Here Paul prays that we would be filled with knowledge, spiritual wisdom, and understanding *(v. 9)*. In verse 10, he reveals what this spiritual knowledge (theology) will bring about. Read verse 10 again, looking for what Paul hopes will come to be as a result of his prayer for spiritual wisdom. Jot down what you see. (Check out the cheat sheet if you get stuck!)

(1) Walk worthy of the Lord
(2) Be fruitful in every good work
(3) Increase in Gods Knowledge

Our theology matters because what we believe affects everything about us. Everything.

You might think you know nothing about theology, but even if you haven't stepped foot in a seminary class, you hold beliefs about God. You have a theology. You might not realize you do, and you may not be able to articulate it, but you have beliefs about God, and your theology is always shaping your experiences.

Many Christians measure spiritual growth by actions. I used to. Behavior modification was my go-to. Good works were my measuring stick. The problem is, actions can be altered without any change of heart. Exhibit A: the Pharisees. From the outside, they looked like really, really holy people. They knew God's Law backward and forward, but their hearts were far from Him and Jesus rebuked them for it *(Matthew 15:7–8)*.

I've come to realize that those who are spiritual-looking are not always those who are spiritually thriving. Attending church, knowing all the Sunday School answers, even reading my Bible every day, doesn't mean that I am growing spiritually. Those who are truly in a flourishing relationship with God are those whose view of God is continually growing bigger. Most problems that ail my soul and negatively affect my actions stem back to a faulty belief about myself, God, or both. If my view of Him is small, weak, distant, or disinterested, I will have no choice but to give into fear, anxiety, control, and manipulation.

Once we learn to focus on righting our beliefs about God, instead of solely righting our wrongs, a radical shift occurs, leading to obedient acts of worship. We want our lives to accurately reflect the holiness our Savior has granted us. We study our Bible because we want to learn more about God. We want to be with God's people to talk about His goodness, learn more about Him, and worship Him together. And as we continually conform our minds to the truths we learn about God through studying and hearing the Word of God preached, our view of Him grows bigger and bigger, resulting in a genuine worship welling up within our souls that accompanies a power that no list-making can provide.

*{God, open my eyes to behold You as You really are. I know that my sight is limited and my focus diverted from the reality of Your goodness and glory. Show me who You are. Make my knowledge of You grow bigger and bigger in such a way that it will move me toward a faith that draws nearer and nearer to You.}*

# *Bonus Study*

Look up the following verses, and note what you learn about God. For an even deeper study, follow the cross-references for each verse to reveal even more truths about God. Take some time to evaluate your current portrait of God and how it lines up with what the Bible says about God.

Psalm 90:2

Psalm 139:7–10

Daniel 2:21

John 14:6

Hebrews 6:17

James 1:17

1 John 4:8

Revelation 4:8

Write out Colossians 3:1–4 in your favorite translation onto a few 3-by-5 cards. Keep the verses with you, post them around your house, and commit them to memory.

# Cheat Sheet

4. Take a quick peek at Colossians 1:9–10. Here Paul prays that we would be filled with knowledge, spiritual wisdom, and understanding *(v. 9)*. In verse 10, he reveals what this spiritual knowledge (theology) will bring about. Read verse 10 again, looking for what Paul hopes will come to be as a result of his prayer for spiritual wisdom. Jot down what you see.

   *walk in a manner worthy of the Lord*
   *be fully pleasing to God*
   *bear fruit in every good work*
   *increase in the knowledge of God*

# Observation

## FOCUSing on Colossians 3:1–4

*Not having a righteousness of my own that comes from the law, but that which comes through faith in Christ, the righteousness from God that depends on faith. –Philippians 3:9*

**I DARESAY CANCER** has affected all mankind. If it hasn't touched you personally, it has invaded a family member or friend. One of my earliest brushes with cancer was my sophomore year at Auburn University when my friend Jill was diagnosed with leukemia. She had to quit her classes and return home to Texas to receive the cancer-stopping treatments. In her case, killing the cancer wasn't enough. She needed a stem-cell transplant to replace the rogue cells the treatment had killed off. Stem cells are the precursors to every vital blood cell required to survive. When the chemo knocked out the cancer, it also removed the cells needed to produce red blood cells, white blood cells, and platelets, all of which are necessary to sustain life. Since she had an identical twin sister, Jill's case couldn't have been any more ideal, and her body successfully received and accepted the new stem cells. These gifted cells have replicated again and again and provide life to her body to this day.

While cancer and disease threaten our physical bodies, we each inherited a spiritual disease from the fall of Adam: a sin-stained soul. Through him sin and death entered the world, and we've all been infected with a cancer of spirit no earthy treatment can fix.

In yesterday's studies we chatted about the importance of our view of God. Besides the character of our God, there is no greater truth to understand than our position in Christ—the truths about who we are now because of the work of Christ on our behalf. The Cross of Christ changed everything for us, and this week's passage holds some very important foundational truths we need to sink deep down into our souls.

1. Open your time with God by writing a prayer in the space below, expressing your thankfulness for Christ's provision on the Cross. Ask the Holy Spirit for His wisdom and revelation as we dive deeper into the truths held in these verses.

## *Look at the Details*

2. Read Colossians 3:1–4. In the following chart, note what these verses teach about what is true of you because of the actions of Christ. (Check out the cheat sheet at the end of today's study if you get stuck.)

## Truths About Me

I died to myself
I am Hidden in Christ
I was raised to new life in Jesus
I need to set my mind on Heaven
When Jesus returns Im going
home w/ Him + I'll be glorified!

All of this is only the tip of the iceberg. The Word of God is filled with truth after truth of the transformation that begins the moment of our salvation. There were immediate revolutions that occurred (justification), there are reformations that are currently in process (sanctification), and there are renewals that will be completed when we meet Jesus face-to-face (glorification). Each stage is part of our complete salvation from sin, and all of them should affect our everyday devotion to our Savior. (For a deeper study of these stages of our salvation, check out my Bible study *Everyday Hope*.)

3. Take a peek back at the truths you listed above. Rewrite them in the appropriate columns in the following chart. Pay attention to the verbs used in each. Do they point to something that has been in the past? Are now in the present? Will be in the future?

| Past | Present | Future |
| --- | --- | --- |
| Ive been raised w/ Christ. Ive died w/ Christ | My Life is hidden w/ Christ | I will appear w/ Christ in glory! |

4. Read Colossians 3:1–4 again, this time looking for any commands.

| Commands Given |
| --- |
| Set my mind on things above<br>Seek things above |

So what does this all mean?

Romans 6:23 tells us the wages of sin—what we each earn because of our sins—is spiritual death, meaning eternal separation from God. We read in Colossians 3:3 that we have died with Christ. When Christ suffered and died on the Cross, He took on our sins. When He died, the penalty of our sins was paid. The sin-sick part of each of us died with Christ. Not only did we die with Christ but also

we were raised with Him. "Even when we were dead in our trespasses, [God] made us alive together with Christ—by grace you have been saved" *(Ephesians 2:5)*. When Christ rose from the grave, He defeated the power of sin and death, and the same part of us that died with Christ was also made alive with Christ. We are forever linked with the death and resurrection of Christ through our salvation.

I am in Christ and His righteousness is in me. I am forever changed. I am no longer defined by my failure. "I have been crucified with Christ. It is no longer I who live, but Christ who lives in me" *(Galatians 2:20)*. Therefore, God is not standing in disapproval of me, because He sees me as the new creation I am. Holy. Blameless. Loved. This is only possible because, through Christ, the penalty of my sin was paid for and removed from me, as far as the east is from the west *(Psalm 103:12)*. When God looks at me, He sees me through the righteousness of Christ and therefore looks on me with approval and love and great, great grace.

The truths in Colossians 3 are crucial to our everyday understanding of obedience: I have died with Christ and have been raised from the dead with Christ. Christ not only defeated my soul-cancer, He gave me new life through imputing His perfect righteousness to me. "For our sake he made him to be sin who knew no sin, so that in him we might become the righteousness of God" *(2 Corinthians 5:21)*. Christ's sacrifice on the Cross wasn't just a merciful act of wiping my slate clean. Once my sins were paid for, His Resurrection brought new life, and His complete obedience brought me right standing with God. And now, when God looks at me He no longer sees my sin-stained soul. Instead, He sees His Son's perfect righteousness.

"And you, who once were alienated and hostile in mind, doing evil deeds, [Christ] has now reconciled in his body of flesh by his death, in order to present you holy and blameless and above reproach before him" *(Colossians 1:21–22)*. I don't always understand it. It blows my mind, actually. But this truth about how God now sees me, because I have died and been raised with Christ, is a pivotal truth for each of us to hold on to. And when we get it—really get it—worship-filled obedience becomes the right response to work of Christ.

> *Because the sinless Savior died,*
>
> *My sinful soul is counted free.*
>
> *For God the just is satisfied,*
>
> *To look on Him and pardon me.*
>
> —CHARITIE L. BANCROFT, "BEFORE THE THRONE OF GOD ABOVE," 1863

*{God, open my heart to these truths. Give me a deep hold–an unshakeable belief–that You see me through Christ's perfection. Show me how I can walk in confidence in these truths. I am accepted. I am beloved. You are pleased with me because of Christ. Stir up within me a great desire to honor and worship You with my every attitude and action, in response to this grace You've given me.}*

## *Bonus Study*

Study 1 Peter 1:3–5; Ephesians 1:3–14; and/or Romans 8:1–17. Add to your list from question 2 of today's study of what is true of you because of Christ.

Continue your memory work on Colossians 3:1–4.

# Cheat Sheet

2. Read Colossians 3:1–4. In the following chart, note what these verses teach about what is true of you because of the actions of Christ.

### Truths About Me

I have been raised with Christ (v. 1)
I have died with Christ (v. 3)
my life is hidden with Christ (v. 3)
Christ is my life (v. 4)
I will appear with Christ in glory (v. 4)

3. Take a peek back at the truths you listed above. Rewrite them in the appropriate columns in the following chart. Pay attention to the verbs used in each. Do they point to something that has been in the past? Are now in the present? Will be in the future?

| Past | Present | Future |
| --- | --- | --- |
| I have been raised with Christ (v. 1)<br>I have died with Christ (v. 3) | my life is hidden with Christ (v. 3)<br>Christ is my life (v. 4) | I will appear with Christ in glory (v. 4) |

4. Read Colossians 3:1–4 again, this time looking for any commands.

### Commands Given

seek the things that are above (v. 1)
set your mind on things that are above (v. 2)

# Clarification

## FOCUSing on Colossians 3:1–4

*My sheep hear my voice, and I know them, and they follow me. I give them eternal life, and they will never perish, and no one will snatch them out of my hand. –John 10:27–28*

**I'VE BEEN OBSESSED** with historical fiction lately. I finally learned how to get audiobooks from the library downloaded to my phone, and now every moment of idle time, I'm listening to something new. Most of my favorites have been narratives set in World War II. I've learned more about World War II from these books than any history class. This is not an offense to my high school teachers or college history professor, instead it attests to the power of story. I'm hooked.

Through these books, I'm learning the importance of the paperwork of the time. The Germans were meticulous record keepers, and every person was to be accounted for, along with many details about them. Their demographics (most important of which was their race), military position (if any), and travel permissions were all on their papers. If someone lost their papers, trouble followed. To avoid unnecessary attention or arrest, people of those days learned to keep their identity papers accessible, yet in a safe place.

Though not as imminently important, since we typically have some sort of digital backup, we too have papers and possessions we hide for safe-keeping. Birth certificates, car titles, property deeds, jewelry appraisals, wills, and marriage certificates are typically all hidden from everyday living. They are important documents, in need of protecting. Many tell who we are and what we're worth, in an earthly sense.

Through Christ, we have a new identity. It, too, is in a safe place, hidden with Christ. "But our citizenship is in heaven, and from it we await a Savior, the Lord Jesus Christ" *(Philippians 3:20)*. We were forever fused into the family of God, and Christ is our deed, our certificate, our proof of citizenship in the kingdom of God.

1. Open your study time with prayer. Thank God for the security you have because you are "in Christ." Ask Him to help you understand this truth in a deeper way today.

## *Uncover the Original Meaning*

As part of our Clarification day, we come to our Greek study. You may be a bit intimidated by the thought of studying the original language, but it's an important layer we get to peel back. With the right tools, studying the Greek can be as simple as looking up a word in the dictionary. If this is your first attempt at Greek study or you need a refresher, I encourage you to check out the videos I've created to show you how to use many of the online Greek tools. Head to KatieOrr.me/Resources, and look for the Videos section.

**DECIDE which word you would like to study.**

2. To start your Greek study, look for any potential keywords in Colossians 3:1–4. As you find any repeated word or words that seem important to the passage, write them below.

Hidden - Keep out of sight / Concealed
Secret

Appears - Come into sight, become visable

Maybe you had the word *hidden* from verse 3 in your list? Let's study this word together.

**DISCOVER that word as it was originally written.**

Now that you know what you want to study, you need to look up the word *hidden* to find out what the original Greek word is. An interlinear Bible will show you English verses and line up each word next to the Greek words they were translated from. You can find these tools in print form, but the easiest way to use them is through the many free online websites and/or smartphone applications I've listed on my website. Many of these resources will make this step easy to do. You can find the Greek word with a click of a button or tap on the screen.

3. Using your preferred tool, see if you can find the original word for *hidden*, and write it below.

**HIDDEN =** Kryptō - hide one's self Keep Secrect, Secretly hidden

You might have written ***kryptō***, or even ***κρύπτω***. The latter is the original Greek word. Most people (including me!) cannot read this, so an English spelling (known as a transliteration) is typically provided. That is where we get ***kryptō***.

For a more detailed explanation of what is going on behind the scenes of your app or website tool, check out How to Do a Greek Word Study in the appendix.

**DEFINE that word.**

Now that you know the original word for *hidden* used in Colossians 3:3 is ***κρύπτω/kryptō***, we can look up this Greek word to better define and uncover the original meaning. For this, we will fill in the following chart.

**Greek Word:** Hidden
*KRYPTŌ*

**Verse and Version:**
*COLOSSIANS 3:3 ESV*

| Part of Speech: *(verb, noun, etc.)* | Translation Notes: *(How else is it translated? How often is this word used?)* |
|---|---|
| verb | hidden (10x), hid (6x), covered (1x), secretly (1x), hide (1x) |
| **Strong's Concordance Number:** #2928 | **Definition:** keep safe, protect, hide |

Notes:

"hide, for the purpose of safe keeping"

4. Now, why don't you try it on your own? Use the steps we just followed together to look up the word *seek* in verse 1, and fill in the chart provided on the following page. (If you are brand new to Bible study, this may be overwhelming. That's OK. It was for me, as well. Just give it a try, and if you're not up for looking up Greek, choose a few words to look up in the dictionary, and write out their definitions. This is still a great way to do our Clarification work of better understanding the meaning of each word.)

Seek

**Greek word:** Zētēō

**Verse and Version:** Colo 3:1

| Part of Speech: *(verb, noun, etc.)* | Translation Notes: *(How else is it translated? How often is this word used?)* |
|---|---|
| Verb | Seek (100x) Seek for (5x) go about (4x) desire (3x) |
| **Strong's Concordance Number:** | **Definition:** |
| G2212 | Seek, Seek for |

Notes: Seek in order to find
A) To Seek a thing
B) To Seek in order to find out by thinking meditating & reasoning
C) to Seek after, aim at & strive
A) To crave something from some one.

5. What discoveries did you make through your Clarification study?

We are Hidden in God's grace & Love for us.
We Seek God but He also Seeks us.

The Bible spells out much that we have to hope for. First Peter 1:3–5 states this clearly: "Blessed be the God and Father of our Lord Jesus Christ! According to his great mercy, he has caused us to be born again to a living hope through the resurrection of Jesus Christ from the dead, to an inheritance that is imperishable, undefiled, and

unfading, kept in heaven for you, who by God's power are being guarded."

Until we see Him face-to-face in heaven, all that is true of us because of the Cross is hidden with Christ and will one day be revealed fully. Christ Himself made this promise of security in John 10. "I give them eternal life, and they will never perish, and no one will snatch them out of my hand. My Father, who has given them to me, is greater than all, and no one is able to snatch them out of the Father's hand" *(John 10:28–29)*.

*{God, I am so thankful for the great and precious promises You've given me. You are strong and faithful, my trustworthy Shepherd who will never leave me nor forsake me. Remind my heart continually: I am safe in Your hands.}*

## *Bonus Study*

Follow the Greek study steps for additional words in Colossians 3:1–4 as time allows. Feel free to simply look up the definition for the Greek word, especially if this is your first try. There is much to be learned even in that!

Review your memory work. Consider writing out Colossians 3:1–4 again to help ingrain it into your memory.

# Cheat Sheet

4. Look up the word *seek* in verse 1, and fill in the chart.

**Greek Word:** ZĒTEŌ

**Verse and Version:** COLOSSIANS 3:1 ESV

| Part of Speech: *(verb, noun, etc.)* | Translation Notes: *(How else is it translated? How often is this word used?)* |
|---|---|
| verb | used 116 times in ESV<br>95 of those translated as seek/sought |
| Strong's Concordance Number: #2212 | Definition: seek, seek for |

Notes:

(1) to seek in order to find. (1a) to seek a thing. (1b) to seek [in order to find out] by thinking, meditating, reasoning, to enquire into. (1c) to seek after, seek for, aim at, strive after.

# Utilization

## FOCUSing on Colossians 3:1–4

*We were buried therefore with him by baptism into death, in order that, just as Christ was raised from the dead by the glory of the Father, we too might walk in newness of life. —Romans 6:4*

**SOME DEAR FRIENDS** of ours had their first baby boy a few weeks ago. Sweet baby Maverick arrived without any complications on a warm Saturday morning. By Monday, however, the signs of jaundice began to show. Jaundice occurs when the rate of dying red blood cells is too much for the baby's liver to filter. When red cells die, their membranes disintegrate, and all the building blocks of the cells are left in the bloodstream for the liver to filter out and dispose of all the parts. If the rate of dying red cells is too much for the liver to handle, the toxic remnants of the red cells accumulate and, if not taken care of, could lead to problems.

Baby Maverick's jaundice, though it is something they're watching and treating, is a sign of an internal transformation that has occurred in the infant. It means the blood cells that dominated his blood stream so far are now dying to make way for the new "adult" red blood cells he needs for his new environment. In this case, the death of his cells is a good thing. The type of cells needed *in utero* differ from what is needed outside the protection of a mother's womb. A fetus' cells essentially steal oxygen from the mother's cells in the umbilical cord, but they are not best suited for grabbing oxygen from the lungs.

The death of the fetal red cells brings a freedom from mom. Though this freedom may lead to a bit of nostalgia from mom, it is what's best for the baby. A baby *in utero* has no choice of where to go, what to do, what to eat or drink. When the baby is born, its former way of living is gone forever. Without this death and subsequent freedom, the baby is not able to grow toward an independent life.

We too have experienced a new birth. Of course, we were all physically born and have undergone the transition all newborn babies do. However, as Christians, we've experienced a spiritual birth, and with it, a death to our old self. This death brought us freedom from sin. I was a slave to sin, which means I had no choice but to sin *(Romans 6:17, 20)*. Christ purchased us out of this slavery, and we are now free to choose obedience to Christ.

1. Spend some time praising God for His deliverance of your soul from death. Thank Him for your new birth. Ask Him for eyes to see those around you who are in need of spiritual rebirth and how you can be a part of bringing the life-giving good news of Jesus to them.

# *Discover the Connections*

2. Read Colossians 3:1–4 to start your study today.

It's time for our Utilization study, where we'll simply look up verses related to any word or phrase we want to learn more about. To do this, you can use the cross-referencing letters in your study Bible or online study tool. You can also use a Bible dictionary to look up people, places, and themes in the Bible. If your Bible doesn't have cross-references, no worries, there are many free online tools and smartphone apps. Check out my resources page at KatieOrr.me /Resources for a list of cross-referencing tools. Plus, I'll always start you out with a few suggestions for your study.

3. Let's start with the phrase "you have died" in Colossians 3:3. Look up the following references, and take note of any truths that reveal a bigger picture of the threads this verse is attached to. You might consider applying one or more of the FOCUS method steps to that passage, depending on the time you have for the day. I typically enjoy listing out truths I see, especially those that help me understand the original passage I'm studying. You can write out the passage in the space provided or even look up a Greek word or two in your interlinear Bible. Just do what interests you and what you have time for!

**You have died (v. 3)**

Romans 6:6

My old self is crucified w/ Christ
I am no longer enslaved to sin

Romans 7:4

Through Christ I have died to the law.
I belong to Him who has been raised from the dead.
Jesus did this so I can bear fruit.

1 Peter 2:24

Jesus bore my sins on His body on the Cross
He did this so I would die to sin + live for righteousness
I'm healed through His wounds

I am dead to sin. If you are "in Christ," so are you.

Jesus died to rescue me from the bondage of sin, and I am forever free from its power. This means I now have the choice to cast off sin. Though I was hopelessly entangled and strangled by the dominion of sin in my life, through Christ I have been given a way out and the power to walk away. Yet, like a newborn babe, I fumble my way into this new realm of freedom. I don't always understand or remember that I have a choice not to sin. For so long, sin was my default. But now I have a choice and have the very presence of God within me, ready and waiting to enable the next right choice.

Too often, I forget I have a choice. Though a temptation is strong, I don't have to give in to it. Though sin comes easy, it is not my master.

*{God, thank You for rescuing me from spiritual death and separation from You. I don't always perfectly understand the transformation my soul has gone through, but I am thankful for the extent to which You've gone to provide it for me. May my life today, this week, and for the rest of my days on this earth be a continual journey of worshipful obedience to You.}*

## *Bonus Study*

Look up cross-references for additional phrases in this week's passage that you would like to learn more about. Continue until you need to move on with your day. If your Bible does not have cross-references in it, check out the online cross-referencing recommendations at KatieOrr.me/Resources. You could easily spend two or three days, 15 minutes or more at a time, working through each verse. Remember, these days are simply suggestions. Follow God's leading. If He tells you to slow down and dig deep, go for it!

Continue with your memory work. Truly memorizing this passage will take weeks, if not months. Consider downloading a Bible memory app or creating your own system for keeping your verses organized as you continue to work on recalling these verses.

# Cheat Sheet

3. Let's start with the phrase "you have died" in Colossians 3:3. Look up the following references, and take note of any truths that reveal a bigger picture of the threads this verse is attached to.

**You have died (v. 3)**

Romans 6:6

*My old self was crucified with Christ.*
*My body of sin was brought to nothing.*
*I am no longer enslaved to sin!*

Romans 7:4

*Through Christ, I have died to the law.*
*I belong to Him who has been raised from the dead. (Christ!)*
*Jesus did this so I may bear fruit for God.*

1 Peter 2:24

*Jesus bore my sins in His body on the Cross.*
*He did this so that I would die to sin and live to righteousness.*
*I have been healed through His wounds.*

# Summation

## FOCUSing on Colossians 3:1–4

> *But seek first the kingdom of God and his righteousness, and all these things will be added to you. —Matthew 6:33*

**WITH ALL THE** wisdom of a couple of young twentysomethings, my husband (Chris) and I began looking for houses. We figured out what we could afford (not much), invited Chris's parents to join us (because we had no clue what we were doing), and had an agent line up some houses for us to look at. One house looked to have potential. The price was right. The neighborhood looked to be well-kept, with the charm of old trees lining the streets, and the house was nicely situated at the end of a cul-de-sac. It was a small house, but perfect for the two of us, with just a bit of room to grow.

We eagerly waited as the sales agent fumbled around with the realtor's special key box. First glance, we were thrilled. The yard needed some cleaning up, as it had been vacant for a while, but the open floor plan and fenced-in backyard seemed to be a perfect fit. However, Chris noticed something funny in the kitchen. The floor was slanted. There seemed to be a sudden shift in the slope of the back corner. We easily deduced that something must be wrong with the foundation.

We no longer had any interest in the house.

Our lives can be tidy, and look great from the outside, but if our foundation is weak and broken, it will cause problems everywhere. We often spend so much time trying to make the outside of our lives look good, yet we neglect to understand our foundation. The good news is Jesus, our solid Rock, built a sure foundation of righteousness and faithfulness for us to stand from.

## *Respond to God's Word*

Today, let's take some time to slow down and digest what we've been learning by going through our Summation steps. Remember, this is when we begin to answer the question "How should what I've learned affect me?" To do this we will do three things:

> **1. Identify—**Find the main idea of the passage.
>
> **2. Modify—**Evaluate my beliefs in light of the main idea.
>
> **3. Glorify—**Align my life to reflect the truth of God's Word.

1. Ask God to stir your heart toward application (if He hasn't already!). Spend a few moments committing to God to walk ahead in obedience to all He has shown you this week.

**IDENTIFY—Find the main idea of the passage.**

2. Take a few moments to flip back to each day's study to review what you've learned this week. In the space provided, write out

Colossians 3:1–4 in your own words. Or simply write out what you think the main idea of Colossians 3:1–4 is.

Im raised w/ Christ and need to set my mind on things in heaven. My old self died and I am now hidden in Jesus. Im going w/ Him to Glory!

3. Read a commentary or study Bible to see how your observations from this week line up with the scholars. (You can find links to free online commentary options as well as in-print investment suggestions at KatieOrr.me/Resources.) As you search commentaries, ask God to make clear the meaning of any passages that are fuzzy to you. Record any additional observations below.

**MODIFY—Evaluate my beliefs in light of the main idea.**

Prayerfully journal through the following questions, asking the Spirit of God to enlighten and convict you.

4. Do I focus more on righting my beliefs about God, or righting my wrongs? ?

5. How should the reality that I am "hidden with Christ" kindle my affections for God? He protects me Nothing Can harm me. That He Loves me + that makes me Love Him more.

6. Do I believe that, through the provision of Christ's obedience, I stand righteous before God? Is there anything about the truth that Jesus is my righteousness that is hard to believe? Why do you think that is? Yes,

Yes, because I didnt do anything to earn it!

7. How could believing this truth affect my everyday moments?

Freedom!!!

**GLORIFY—Align my life to reflect the truth of God's Word.**

8. Are there any adjustments I need to make in my thinking about what obedience is? About God's approval of me?

Jesus is my righteousness. He lived the perfect life I could never, ever live. He died the death I deserve, paid the penalty of my sin, and exchanged my sin for his perfection—all so I could be in forever fellowship with God.

This work of Christ on my behalf is the only right foundation for obedience. Through it, my old, sinful self has died and been raised with Christ, and His perfect righteousness has been gifted to me. And so, I already have right-standing before God. My life is now hidden with Christ, securely attached to His faithful and good character. One sweet day, I will appear with Christ in heaven to spend eternity with God. Until then, I must set my mind on things that are above.

*{God, I am eternally grateful for the work of Christ and that You chose me to be Your child. Grant me the strength and grace to continually cling to who I am now because of Christ. Expose any lies I believe about myself. Help me to replace them with truth. For Your glory, I choose to walk this day with my heart firmly planted in the foundation of Your love for me.}*

WEEK
3

RIGHTLY RESPONDING TO GRACE

# Fight the Flesh

FOCUSING ON
**COLOSSIANS 3:5–9**

# Foundation

## FOCUSing on Colossians 3:5–9

> *For I do not understand my own actions. For I do not do what I want, but I do the very thing I hate. –Romans 7:15*

**THERE IS NO** shortage of zombie apocalypse books, movies, and TV shows these days. Their premises are all the same: Something has gone wrong, causing millions of people to die. But even though their souls are gone, something causes their bodies to keep moving and acting out. And it wouldn't be great drama if these zombies were good natured. Nope. These soulless beings are on a relentless rampage to attack the living. Zombies, creepers, walkers—whatever you call them—they are the walking dead. And in everyday zombie narrative, the living must fight the dead.

Last week we looked at the fact we are no longer slaves with no choice but to sin. We are now free from sin's power. Our identity is secure with Christ, and we have been given the righteousness of Christ. Yet, my moments seem to prove otherwise. Though I'm dead to sin, I still sin. Though the Bible tells me sin has no power over me, it sometimes feels like it does. I have a choice, yet the lure of sin seems to overtake me again and again.

What's going on?

The sin within me has been dealt a mortal blow through the death and Resurrection of Christ. It is dead. Yet, like a dangerous zombie, it is a walking dead. And if I do not live on guard, the walking dead will overtake me. They will keep me distracted and disoriented, entangled and entrapped, and ultimately ineffective in my pursuits of worship. Remember, obedience is the right response to God's mercy. And from the foundation of righteousness and power laid for us in Christ, we must recognize and engage the battle within.

Fight the flesh. Exterminate the earthly. Wipe out the walking dead.

1. Start today with confession. Admit the places in your life where you have allowed sin to reign instead of telling it who's boss. Thank God for His forgiveness and grace.

## *Enjoy Every Word*

2. We'll work through our first layer of studying Colossians 3:5–9 by copying the passage into the space provided on the next page. Remember, our Foundation work is designed to help us slow down and begin to grasp what is going on in this passage. There is no right or wrong way to do this. It is simply an exercise of intentionally taking in each word, however you enjoy doing so.

3. Which words or phrases in Colossians 3:5–9 stand out to you?

4. Record any questions you have about this passage. Your questions should be answered by the end of the week, as you continue to study. If not, you'll have an opportunity to consult commentaries.

The moment I put my faith in the work of Christ on my behalf, I was given right-standing before God (justification), and His Spirit began to dwell within me. I was "saved" in an instance, but yet another work of God began in that moment—my sanctification. This is the process of becoming more and more like Christ. It is a work God continues to this day and will be completed when I see Jesus face-to-face (glorification). We have been justified, we are being sanctified, and we will be glorified. Sanctification is the part of God's work we are experiencing today.

My sanctification is a work of God, but I play a role as well. Just as I can stoke a fire or smother it to embers, I can also hinder or help the work of the Holy Spirit within me to make me more like Christ. I can let the chocolate settle in the milk, or I can invite it to fill every part of me with its empowering, transforming presence. I can allow sin to reign in my life, or I can put it to death.

My everyday choices matter. My justification—my right standing before God—is forever sealed in heaven, but the degree to which I look like Jesus on this earth will depend on my participation in or refusal of God's work in my life to remove the presence of sin in my day-to-day actions.

*{Lord, help me! The fight against the walking dead (sin) within me is hard. My sinful desires continually entrap me, and I obey their passions instead of walking each day in obedient worship of You, my Savior. Holy Spirit, enable me to put to death the deeds of the flesh in my life. I am so thankful that, even on my worst days, there is no condemnation for those who are in Christ Jesus.}*

## *Bonus Study*

Study Romans 6:1–11, noting what is true of you through the work of Christ.

Write out Colossians 3:5–9 in your favorite translation onto a few 3-by-5 cards, and begin to commit them to memory.

# Observation

## FOCUSing on Colossians 3:5–9

*For freedom Christ has set us free; stand firm therefore, and do not submit again to a yoke of slavery. —Galatians 5:1*

**AUTOPIA AT DISNEYLAND** was one of my favorite rides as a small child. If you haven't been, you've probably seen or been on a similar car ride. I was thrilled to get into that pint-sized car and drive. I could make the car go forward with the gas pedal and even steer the car left or right.

I didn't notice the track underneath the car. So, though I could steer slightly to the left or right, it was there all along bumping me back and forth, keeping me in the center of the road. And though I did make the car go forward with the gas pedal, there was only one speed: really, really slow. In my six-year-old mind's eye, it was awesome—I was driving! Now, as a well-informed adult, I know that "driving" that little automobile is not at all like driving a real car.

Disney's Autopia and other rides like it give children the illusion of control, enough to let them think they are driving, all the while neatly bringing them along the route set in stone. The kids always make it back to the start of the ride. Sin gives us the same illusion of control. Whether we realize it or not, sin enslaves us and takes us down the same pain-filled road of death. Instead, when we keep in step with the Spirit of God, we can travel down the path that leads to the abundant life Christ promised we can experience.

Either way, at any moment in time, we are riding along one path or the other. And, we are always obedient. We are either obeying God or we are obeying our sinful nature. We are slaves to sin or slaves of God. "Do you not know that if you present yourselves to anyone as obedient slaves, you are slaves of the one whom you obey, either of sin, which leads to death, or of obedience, which leads to righteousness?" *(Romans 6:16)*.

1. Open today's time in a prayer of dependency on the Holy Spirit's leading and teaching. Declare your need for Him and desire to obey and rightly respond to His grace.

## *Look at the Details*

2. As you read Colossians 3:5–9, look for the commands given, and write them below.

3. Now, go back through Colossians 3:5–9, and record the specific sins Paul mentions to put to death/put away/put off.

4. Look back at your list of vices from our passage. Categorize them by any similarities you see in them. (Yours might be slightly different from mine, but you can check out the cheat sheet to see what I came up with.)

In the zombie narratives, some of the living keep their dead in chains. They know the dead are dangerous, but they can't bring themselves to finally let go of them. They're holding on to hope for a cure. They believe they may be reunited with them one day. They are unable to face reality: the thing in front of them is not safe. It does not love them. It wants to destroy them.

I have my own cage of walking dead. My old friends of anger, covetousness, and more. Before I came to Christ, I followed them without thought, enjoying the ride to destruction. But then Christ interrupted the journey. He rescued me from their power and put me on a new road to life. But sometimes (more often than I like to admit), I try to tango with my former captors. Instead of destroying them, I crawl close enough for a quick and harmless indulgence, thinking I can keep them at a safe distance.

Yet one step leads to two, and the next thing I know, I'm in the cage with them. I am once again their puppet. Anger wraps its death grip on my heart, and I follow it down the path of destruction. A part of me deep down knows that my outbursts will only bring pain, sadness, and a wedge between me and the ones I lash out at, but once I'm in the cage, it's hard to get out.

I must put anger to death. Covetousness must die. Pride cannot be let loose. Because the zombies of my old sinful self are constantly wandering inside of me, looking for their time to pounce. "For the desires of the flesh are against the Spirit, and the desires of the Spirit are against the flesh, for these are opposed to each other, to keep you from doing the things you want to do" *(Galatians 5:17)*. There is a war waging within me, and I must be always ready to put up a fight.

*{God, without You, I am defenseless. I am so thankful that Your Spirit lives within me, fighting with me to put to death everything earthly in me. Help me see the danger in entertaining sin. Grant me the resolve to let go of the destructive old friends I want to keep near. Thank You for Your continual grace.}*

## *Bonus Study*

Study Romans 6:15–23, specifically noting what it teaches about obedience and being slaves of sin versus slaves of righteousness.

Continue your memory work on Colossians 3:5–9.

# Cheat Sheet

2. As you read Colossians 3:5–9, look for the commands given, and write them below.

   *put to death what is earthly in you (v. 5)*

   *put them all away (v. 8)*

   *put off the old self (v. 9)*

3. Now, go back through Colossians 3:5–9, and record the specific sins Paul mentions to put to death/put away/put off.

   *sexual immorality, impurity, passion (sexual appetite), evil desire, covetousness (idolatry) (v. 5)*

   *anger, wrath, malice, slander, obscene talk from your mouth (v. 8)*

   *lying (v. 9)*

   *practices of old self (v. 9)*

4. Look back at your list of vices from our passage. Categorize them by any similarities you see in them. (Yours might be slightly different from mine.)

   *Internal Passions: sexual immorality, impurity, passion, evil desire, covetousness*

   *Outbursts: anger, wrath, malice*

   *External Speech: slander, obscene talk, lying*

# Clarification

## FOCUSing on Colossians 3:5–9

**MOST OF MY** life, my dad has owned a boat. I grew up on the lake and learned to water ski when I was four. My siblings and I learned at a young age how to protect Daddy's boat, which is incredibly important because boats have a tendency to drift. If a boat is not attached to the dock, it will float away without fail—even in the smoothest of waters.

The Bible is clear that there are two ways to live—there is no in between. I am either obedient or I am disobedient. I am either chasing after the presence of God, or I am following my flesh. I am tied to the dock, or I'm drifting away. And, as we looked at yesterday, we have many enemies attempting to lure us out into dangerous waters, so we have to purposefully fight to stay tied to the dock of God's presence. One of the sneakiest of sins is our consuming ambitions. They don't start off consuming, of course. They can even start off as well-meaning service to God. But somewhere along the way, our focus shifts from God's will to our will. From He to me.

1. Open today's time with prayer, inviting the Spirit of God to show any areas in your life that have become a consuming distraction from following God with all your heart.

## *Uncover the Original Meaning*

We're back again at the original Greek. I know this day can seem daunting and difficult, especially if this is a new skill for you. Just as learning to ride a bike or figuring out the latest technology can be frustrating at times, the rewards of pressing in and continuing on are worth it! If the thought of studying the Greek is still too much, consider selecting a few words to look up in the dictionary, then rewrite the verse with the definition in place of the word you looked up. Do what works for you, but do try something!

**DECIDE which word you would like to study.**

2. To start your Greek study, look for any potential keywords in Colossians 3:5–9. As you find any repeated word or words that seem important to the passage, write them below.

**DISCOVER that word as it was originally written.**

3. There are many great words to look up, but I want to make sure you look up at least one today: *covetousness*. Using an interlinear Bible, find the original word for *covetousness* used in verse 5, and write it in the space provided.

***COVETOUSNESS =***

**DEFINE that word.**

4. Now we can look up the Greek word for *covetousness* and fill in our chart below. I've filled out some of it for you. Try to fill in the rest.

**Greek word:** *PLEONEXIA*

**Verse and Version:**

| Part of Speech: *(verb, noun, etc.)* Noun | Translation Notes: *(How else is it translated? How often is this word used?)* |
|---|---|
| Strong's Concordance Number: #4124 | Definition: |
| Notes: | |

5. Follow the Greek study steps to look up at least one more word in this week's passage. Here are a couple you might choose from:

***PUT TO DEATH (v. 5)***

***WALKED (v. 7)***

**Greek word:** ______________________

**Verse and Version:** ______________________

| Part of Speech:<br>*(verb, noun, etc.)* | Translation Notes:<br>*(How else is it translated? How often is this word used?)* |
|---|---|
| Strong's Concordance Number: | Definition: |
| Notes: | |

6. What did you discover through your Clarification study? Which word did you learn the most about? (Remember, if you are still not ready to try studying the Greek, feel free to skip all this. Instead, look up the word in the dictionary and write out the definition. Just do something to help you go deeper into the passage we're becoming more and more familiar with.)

In a culture in which we are continually pointed toward self-gratification, I imagine I'm not the only one reading this who struggles with covetousness. We probably wouldn't call it coveting, but Paul helps us understand what he means by covetousness through the last clause at the end of verse 5: "which is idolatry." *Ouch.*

My guess is, you don't have miniature figurines of other gods around your house. But we all have things, people, and desires we put before God.That's an idol, anything we want more than we want God.These idols can be good things, good people. Our friends. Our kids. Our job. Even our pursuits for God. Idolatry comes easily, and yet it often goes unrecognized in our lives.

I need to regularly take a good look at what consumes me. Is it God's presence? God's plan? God's purposes? Or am I consumed with my plans, my purposes, and my pursuits for significance, acceptance, and the adoration of others? All too often, I spend too much time looking around to all others have, and when I see all they have (and I don't), I am driven by the ambition to pursue what they have and that often leads right into idolatry. As I keep my eyes on Christ, however, those consuming passions fade away.

*{God, help me recognize what I am holding on to more tightly than I ought to. Show me the places in my heart that crave something or someone more than I crave You. Give me an overwhelming desire to be with You and a brokenness over my sin of idolatry. Holy Spirit, enable me to let go of my covetousness, turn from my idols, and run to You.}*

# *Bonus Study*

Follow the Greek study steps for additional words in Colossians 3:5–9 as time allows.

Review your memory work. Consider writing out Colossians 3:5–9 again to help ingrain it into your memory.

# Cheat Sheet

3. Using an interlinear Bible, find the original word for *covetousness* used in verse 5, and write it in the space provided.

**COVETOUSNESS = πλεονεξία = PLEONEXIA**

4. Now we can look up the Greek word for *covetousness* and fill in our chart below.

**Greek word:** *PLEONEXIA*

**Verse and Version:** *COLOSSIANS 3:5 ESV*

| Part of Speech: *(verb, noun, etc.)* | Translation Notes: *(How else is it translated? How often is this word used?)* |
|---|---|
| noun | covet/covetousness (10x), greed (3x), greedy (1x), exaction (1x) (ESV usage) |
| Strong's Concordance Number: #4124 | Definition: greediness, greed |

Notes:

"It is the longing for something that belongs to someone else or placing supreme value on something not (yet) possessed. As used in this context, it is a serious sin; and Paul no doubt included it because it is, in kind, the same as sexual sin. It represents a strong movement of desire toward something out of God's will at the time." —Richard R. Melick, *Philippians, Colossians, Philemon*, Vol. 32, The New American Commentary

# Utilization

## FOCUSing on Colossians 3:5–9

*But put on the Lord Jesus Christ, and make no provision for the flesh, to gratify its desires. –Romans 13:14*

**BY GOD'S GREAT** mercy, the Orr household has evaded head lice. Several friends and family members have had a visit from these nasty little creatures, and every time a lice invasion occurs, I've noticed they all engage in the same strategy to rid themselves of the infestation: *You're going down, lice.*

Project Take Down is no joke. All sheets and clothes are washed with very hot water. All heads in the household are sanitized with a special shampoo, followed by a careful inspection. Strand by strand, hair is checked for the bugs and their teeny-tiny eggs. Special combs are used to pull out the nits. Anything that might be infected but can't be washed goes in the freezer. There is a lethal determination involved in Project Take Down. No rest for the weary. No stone goes unturned. No bug receives mercy. Because the person knows (mostly because of experience) that if they don't get every bug and their eggs, the lice will return.

Even more so, we are to treat our sin with the same disgust and desertion. Project Take Down must be continually employed. With the same careful inspection and lethal determination, our old sinful patterns must be put to death.

1. Spend some time in prayer. Ask God to show you the sin you've allowed to settle in and colonize in your day-to-day life. Confess any areas of sin brought to mind. Thank Him for His continual, unending mercy and grace.

## *Discover the Connections*

2. Read Colossians 3:5–9 to start your study today.

3. Following are cross-references for several of the key phrases in our passage. Look up the verses, and note anything connected to the truths found in Colossians 3.

**put to death (v. 5)**

Romans 8:13

Galatians 5:24

**what is earthly in you (v. 5)**

Romans 6:13–14

**put them all away (v. 8)**

Ephesians 4:22

Project Take Down begins with admitting there's a problem. If head lice don't bother you, there's no need to turn the house upside down to get rid of them. But if they disgust you, it's all hands on deck. Part of our sanctification (becoming more like Jesus) process is seeing our sin for what it really is. Disgusting. Dangerous. Destructive. Repulsion of our sin is a natural fruit of our salvation. When we grasp the true repugnant state of our sinful deeds, especially compared to the new righteousness we've been given through Christ, Project Take Down should be the only option. "Let us also lay aside every weight, and sin which clings so closely, and let us run with endurance the race that is set before us" *(Hebrews 12:1).*

*{God, open my eyes to the reality of my sin. Show me where I've let it run rampant within me. Give me the resolve to put it to death and continually put it away from me. For Your glory.}*

## *Bonus Study*

Look up cross-references for additional phrases in Colossians 3:5–9 that you would like to learn more about. If your Bible does not have cross-references in it, check out the free online cross-referencing tool recommendations at KatieOrr.me/Resources.

Continue with your memory work of Colossians 3:5–9. Add your verses to your memory review system.

# Cheat Sheet

3. Following are cross-references for several of the key phrases in our passage. Look up the verses, and note anything connected to the truths found in Colossians 3.

**put to death (v. 5)**

Romans 8:13

*living according to the flesh leads to death*

*putting to death the deeds of the body (by the power of the Spirit) leads to life*

Galatians 5:24

*those who belong to Christ Jesus have crucified the flesh with its passions and desires*

**what is earthly in you (v. 5)**

Romans 6:13–14

*Truths About Me: I have been brought from death to life, sin will have no dominion over me, I am not under law but under grace*

*Commands: I am not to use my body for unrighteousness and sin, I am to present myself to God, I am to use my body as an instrument for righteousness*

**put them all away (v. 8)**

Ephesians 4:22

*Truths About My Old Self: belongs to my former manner of life, is corrupt through deceitful desires*

*Command: put off my old self*

# Summation

## FOCUSing on Colossians 3:5–9

*And everyone who thus hopes in him purifies himself as he is pure. —1 John 3:3*

**SUMMERS IN THE** Orr household are spent at the local pool. With a large deep end, water slide, and kiddie playground near the ground entrance, it's fun for all ages. Little ones are expected to have swim diapers on. Though we are past that stage of life, I am thankful they are required, or else our pool time would be interrupted often. If a toddler violates the pool by taking a twosies without a swim diaper on, pool time is shut down, and the lifeguards follow a protocol to cleanse the pool from the contaminate. Can you imagine what swim time would be like if there were no potty-at-the-pool etiquette or way to clean the mess up?

At first, I hesitated to use this analogy because the thought of swimming in poo is disgusting and probably offensive to you. Yet, I think the repulsion this image gives is just a fraction of the aversion we should have to our sin. Not one of us would jump into a pool with excrement floating around in it. The thought of it is downright disgusting. Yet, how much more detestable is our sin?

We must defend the purity of our pool.

Sin is a disgusting contamination—a violation—of the righteousness Christ died to provide for us. Until we meet Jesus face-to-face in heaven, our lives will be constantly threatened by the contamination of sin. And if we aren't vigilant to protect our lives from the pollutants, poisons, and profanities that daily threaten our purity, what was meant to be a shining display of the beauty and righteousness of Christ becomes a cesspool of decay and disease. Our hearts and minds, and therefore our attitudes and behavior, will reek of death instead of being the fragrant aroma of Christ.

"Since we have these promises, beloved, let us cleanse ourselves from every defilement of body and spirit, bringing holiness to completion in the fear of God" *(2 Corinthians 7:1)*. Our position in Christ—as holy and beloved—is forever secure. Our becoming like Christ is still in progress. As we choose obedience—again and again and again—our inner truths become outward realities. No amount of pollution can change our identities as children of God, but our worship of Him is worked out as we keep our lives clean. Cleaning our lives is not meant to be a chore or a burden. Purifying our lifestyles is a natural outpouring of our desire to honor God, be like Christ, and allow our lives to reflect the glorious righteousness provided for us.

## *Respond to God's Word*

1. Write out a prayer to prepare your heart, asking God to clearly show you what actions to take in response to your studies. Ask Him to give you a deepening desire to walk in holiness.

**IDENTIFY—Find the main idea of the passage.**

2. Take a few moments to flip back to each day's study to review what you've learned this week. In the space provided, write out Colossians 3:5–9 in your own words. Or simply write out what you think the main idea of Colossians 3:5–9 is, in regard to our study of obedience.

3. Read a commentary or study Bible to see how your observations line up with the scholars. (You can find links to free commentary options as well as in-print investment suggestions at KatieOrr.me/Resources.) As you search commentaries, ask God to make clear the meaning of any passages that are fuzzy to you. Record any additional observations below.

**MODIFY—Evaluate my beliefs in light of the main idea.**

Prayerfully journal through the following questions, asking the Spirit of God to enlighten and convict you.

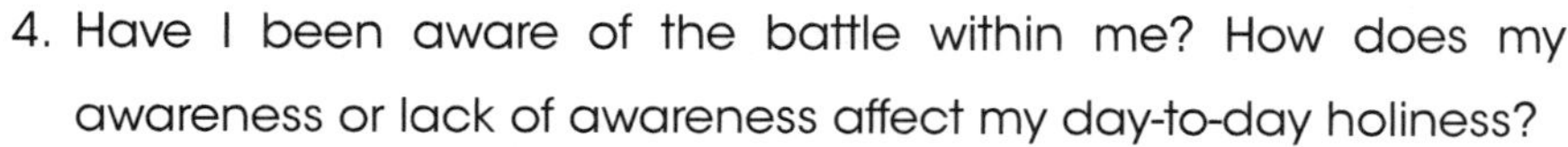

4. Have I been aware of the battle within me? How does my awareness or lack of awareness affect my day-to-day holiness?

5. Do I take my sin seriously? Does my heart grieve deeply when I sin? Why, or why not?

6. How actively engaged am I in Project Take Down? Circle below the best representation of your efforts to remove sinful habits from your life.

   *(0=sin is running rampant, 10=constantly on guard, ready to kill sinful deeds)*

   1 • • • • 2 • • • • 3 • • • • 4 • • • • 5 • • • • 6 • • • • 7 • • • • 8 • • • • 9 • • • • 10

**GLORIFY—Align my life to reflect the truth of God's Word.**

7. Which of the vices in Colossians 3:5–9 do I most need to wage war against?

8. What steps do I need to take, in order, toward Project Take Down?

*{God, I praise You that even when I was dead in my nasty transgressions, You came to rescue me. Thank You for drawing me up from the pit, out of the deep mess I was in. I confess that I keep returning to that mess. Something about it is comfortable and gratifying, but I know it only brings destruction to me and those around me. Most importantly, it draws me away from You. Holy Spirit, help me to walk away from the sin that so easily entangles me. Show me what it looks like for me to lay it aside today. I am desperate for the change that only You can bring. I praise You for Your great, great, glorious grace.}*

RIGHTLY RESPONDING TO GRACE

# Walk in Holiness

FOCUSING ON
**COLOSSIANS 3:10–17**

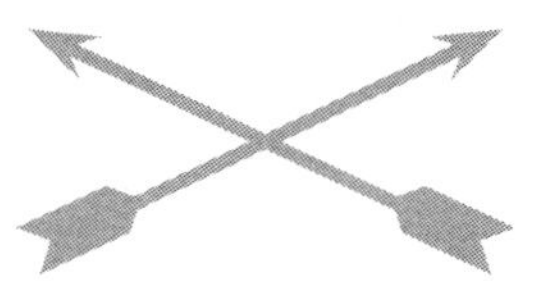

# Foundation

## FOCUSing on Colossians 3:10–17

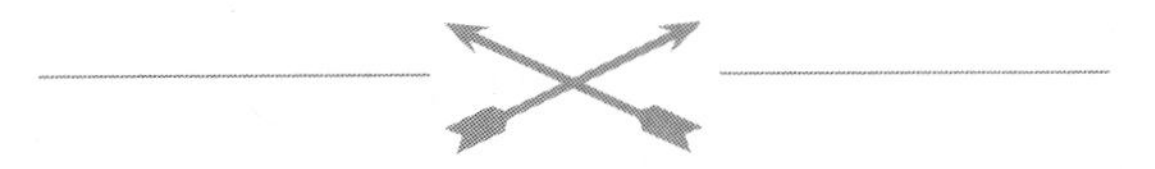

*Therefore, if anyone is in Christ, he is a new creation. The old has passed away; behold, the new has come. —2 Corinthians 5:17*

**I'VE BEEN TO** the Grand Canyon twice, and both trips were way too quick. My first trip was a three-week, cross-country family motorhome trek when I was a disinterested teenager. Though I was way to cool to show it at the time, I loved that trip. We played cards, read books, visited many national narks, and frequented the fun KOAs—Kampgrounds of America. When we made it to the Grand Canyon and beheld its vast beauty, my mind had a very difficult time processing its tremendousness. It was bigger and grander than anything I had ever seen, so much so that it seemed fake to my 15-year-old brain. Of course, I could literally see that it was real—the depth and detail were undeniable—but it was as if my mind could not handle the grandeur. When my parents asked me what I thought about the sight, I told them I thought it looked like cardboard; like a painted facade at the theme park Knott's Berry Farm. That was all my mind had to compare it to.

My second trip to the Grand Canyon lasted a mere hour. Chris and I were heading home from a trip to Colorado. My first niece had been born that morning, and though we couldn't wait to get home to see my sister and the new baby, we simply couldn't pass up stopping at the Grand Canyon along the way. It was a last-minute decision, but we made it to the park about an hour before sundown. We soaked up as much of its golden-hour glory as we could, and I was yet again—10 years later—struck by the depth and breadth of the canyon.

The Grand Canyon is up to one mile deep and, at its widest point, 18 miles wide. Even the best Olympic long jumper could not make it across the Grand Canyon. He or she may be able to jump much farther than I ever could, but our fate would be the same. Neither of us would make it across.

No one can make it across the Grand Canyon by his or her jumping efforts alone. Nor can we make it across the infinitely greater divide that separates mankind from God. The Cross of Christ alone can bridge that great gap. Sure, there are people on this earth who look better, pray better, study their Bible better, and are all-around more obedient than the average Joe, but even their best attempts to reach God on their own are like trying to jump across the Grand Canyon. Impossible. Insufficient. Insanity.

We must be careful not to turn our obedience into an effort to shorten the gap between us and God. The colossal rift has already been mercifully bridged, and the deep chasm has been filled with His all-sufficient grace. We don't have to obey God to keep His favor. Instead, we get to live out our lives as a response to His grace—as "God's chosen ones, [already] holy and beloved" *(Colossians 3:12)*.

God's Grand Canyon bridge of grace deserves our Grand Canyon worship—an awe-filled, grateful adoration that brings us to our knees in praise. And the more we understand the depths of His Grand Canyon-crossing rescue and the riches that He has poured out on us, the more we might just find ourselves without words to accurately describe the grandeur of our Rescuer.

1. Ask God to open your eyes to better see the reality of His Grand Canyon rescue of your soul. With Grand Canyon worship, write out a prayer of praise, lift up your voice in song, and/or raise your hands in worship to Him.

## *Enjoy Every Word*

2. Once again, for our Foundation day, we'll work through the first layer of this week's section of Colossians 3:10–17. Write out the passage below.

3. Which words or phrases in Colossians 3:10–17 stand out to you?

4. Record any questions you have about this passage.

Sometimes I revert back to a 15-year-old view of the glory of God's rescue of my soul. The grace of God becomes flat and lifeless in my mind's eye. The depth of my depravity before Christ doesn't look so deep. The triumph of my rescue doesn't seem all that monumental. But when I slow down and allow my heart and mind to marinate in "the breadth and length and height and depth" *(Ephesians 3:18)* of Christ's love for me, my soul can't help but break out in Grand Canyon-sized worship. Why God would choose to save this wretched soul is beyond me, but I am eternally grateful.

And so, I live a therefore life. I have been rescued and redeemed, therefore, I choose to obey. I have been forgiven and pardoned, therefore, I will forgive the unpardonable in others. I have been loved sacrificially by God, therefore, I will enduringly love others. I have been made holy and blameless, therefore, I choose to live up to that standard. I live a life of response to God's Grand Canyon rescue plan.

Do you see how remembering the work of Christ and all that means for us is key to our everyday obedience? It turns duty into delight. Works into worship. A list of chores into the details of a glorious calling. It's how and why we "do everything in the name of the Lord Jesus, giving thanks to God the Father through him" *(Colossians 3:17)*.

*{God, show me Your glory! Again and again and again, remind me of the pit from which You rescued me. Awaken my mind to the reality of how lost I was without You. Stir my heart's affections toward Grand Canyon worship today. Let me not forget all You have done to make me Your own. Thank You for rescuing me. Thank You for the righteousness of Christ. Thank You for your unconditional love. Thank You for this new calling of holy obedience. May I walk worthy of this calling today, by the power of Your Spirit. Be glorified in me today.}*

## *Bonus Study*

Spend some time in Isaiah 53, a prophecy of the coming Savior. Make a list of all that Christ went through to bring us salvation, then write out a prayer to God, thanking Him for every one of those truths.

Write out Colossians 3:10–17 in your favorite translation on to a few 3-by-5 cards, and commit them to memory this week.

# Observation

## FOCUSing on Colossians 3:10–17

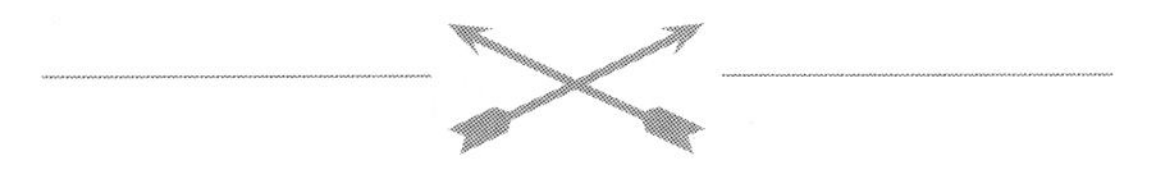

*Put on the new self, created after the likeness of God in true righteousness and holiness. —Ephesians 4:24*

**THE EXPRESSION OF** genetics is fascinating to me. Taking after my mother's side of the family, with dark hair and light eyes, my sister and I look very much alike. Whereas my blonde-haired, blue-eyed brothers received more traits from my father's gene pool. My oldest two children are a sweet mesh of mine and my husband's physical traits. They have my facial features, with his hair and eye colors. My third-born looks nothing like either of us. He's another blonde-headed, blue-eyed boy and looks just like my brothers and my father.

In the physical realm, our DNA dictates who we are. Male or female. 5′1″ or 5′11″. Blonde or brunette. From the size of our bones and the shape of our face to our skin color and blood type, so many details about who we are stem back to a set of proteins, in a particular pattern, that tell our bodies how to express themselves. A wonder, indeed.

When we enter into new life as a Christian, we are given a new spiritual self. That part of us now has a completely new spiritual DNA, and with this new identity a new character begins to emerge, one that reflects the character of Christ. Before Christ, our spiritual DNA was wired to sin. It is all we knew to follow in the footsteps of Adam and Eve and the root of sin they produced in each of us. By nature,

we doubted the character of God, we indulged in the cravings of our hearts, and we were dominated by the depraved pattern of our minds. But when we surrendered to Christ as our Savior, we were given new life, and the DNA of our soul was replaced with the perfection of Christ. Finally, through this spiritual transplant, our lives are able to express the perfection we are called to.

The expression of this new nature in our everyday moments takes time (a lifetime, actually), the power of the Holy Spirit, and our continual cooperation—our obedience. As this internal transformation begins to bring forth a transfiguration of our everyday lives, it is the undeniable proof of our salvation.

1. Open your time with God by recording a prayer in the space below. Praise God for the newness He has gifted you. Declare your intentions to walk throughout today in the newness of life He has provided for you.

## *Look at the Details*

2. As you head back to Colossians 3:10–17 today, let's start first with looking for the words Paul used to describe those who are in Christ. Since verse 10 is the end of a sentence, start observing at verse 9, and record any truths you see that are true of you because of the work of Christ. (Check out the cheat sheet at the end of today's study if you get stuck.)

3. Now, let's look for the commands in the passage. Read Colossians 3:10–17 again, and record all the commands you find.

This is a tall order. But, once again, we see where the truths about who we are positionally in Christ are the platform of our obedience. It's important to recognize that the "put on" in verse 10 is not a command. It's a statement of what has already happened, which we can see when we read the entire sentence, beginning in verse 9. So, since the old self has been put off and our new self put on *(v. 10)*—all through the provision of Christ in the moment we became a Christian—then we obey *(v. 12)*. My old self has already been put off, my new self already put on, therefore I will obey.

The word for "put on" in verse 10 can also be translated "to clothe." The same is true in verse 12. When we came to Christ, we were given a great gift: a brand-new, incorruptible, eternal wardrobe of righteousness. Before Christ, all we had to wear were filthy, sin-stained rags. After Christ, we now have a closet full of everything we need for life and godliness *(2 Peter 1:3)*, the fruit of the Spirit *(Galatians 5:22–23)*, the whole armor of God *(Ephesians 6:11–17)*, and these

new garments of godliness (compassionate heart, kindness, humility, meekness, patience, etc.) to adorn our hearts and lives.

Obedience is choosing to put on our beautiful new righteous attire, for which Jesus lived, died, and defeated death to provide for us. "But showing all good faith, so that in everything they may adorn the doctrine of God our Savior" *(Titus 2:10)*. It's a display of the doctrine of grace to those around us. And as we daily and purposefully dress for the occasion—the continual celebration of His glorious grace—our moments, our days, our lifetime will be filled with the glory of our Savior.

*{Jesus, I'm so grateful for Your provision. Forgive me for neglecting to walk in the newness of life You've provided for me. Holy Spirit, help me to purposefully dress in the righteousness of Christ today.}*

## *Bonus Study*

Look up the following verses, and note the desired results of obedience. What should our lives result in?

1 Peter 2:11–12

Matthew 5:13–16

Philippians 1:9–11

Philippians 2:14–15

Continue your memory work of Colossians 3:10–17.

# Cheat Sheet

2. As you head back to Colossians 3:10–17 today, let's start first with looking for the words Paul used to describe those who are in Christ. Since verse 10 is the end of a sentence, start observing at verse 9, and record any truths you see that are true of you because of the work of Christ.

   *I have put off the old self with its practices (v. 9)*
   *I have put on the new self (v. 10)*
   *my new self is being renewed in knowledge after the image of Christ (v. 10)*
   *the Lord has forgiven me (v. 13)*
   *I am called to the peace of Christ (v. 15)*

3. Now, let's look for the commands in the passage. Read Colossians 3:10–17 again, and record all the commands you find.

   *put on compassionate hearts, kindness, humility, meekness, and patience*
   *bear with one another*
   *forgive each other*
   *put on love*
   *let the peace of Christ rule in your hearts*
   *be thankful*
   *let the Word of Christ dwell in you richly*
   *teach and admonish one another in all wisdom*
   *sing psalms and hymns and spiritual songs, with thankfulness in your hearts to God*
   *whatever you do, in word or deed, do everything in the name of the Lord Jesus, giving thanks to God the Father through Him*

# Clarification

## FOCUSing on Colossians 3:10–17

*Only let your manner of life be worthy of the gospel of Christ. —Philippians 1:27*

**LAST SPRING MY** daughter, Anna, wanted to try out for baseball. We tried our best to make sure our eight-year-old knew what she was getting into, and she wholeheartedly promised us she wanted to play. She was so excited to get her first glove, set of cleats, and uniform. Three games in, she was ready to quit. Though we tried to encourage her toward becoming the ballplayer she initially declared she wanted to be, she was extremely disinterested in improving her swing, completely bored with games and practice, and more interested in the snack bar than the scoreboard.

Since baseball didn't stick with Anna, we've been on the look-out for a different athletic outlet. A friend of mine recently opened a local dance studio featuring hip-hop classes. With the same enthusiasm and promise, Anna declared she wanted to take dance classes. I wasn't sure how she would respond to all the swift moves and complicated routines to memorize, but she's jumped in with both feet and embraced the inner dancer within her. She's practiced faithfully and performed all her new moves for every member of the family. Just today, she told me she wished dance classes were every other day instead of weekly. She can't wait to get back to the dance studio.

Anna may not be a ballplayer, but I think we've found the dancer within her. She has a lot of work and training to do to allow this dancer to fully emerge, but her desire to dance is insatiable.

We have a new self, but just like Anna, we have a lot of work to do to catch up with our calling. The holiness of God is within us. It's an unchangeable identity, but we must learn the new rhythms and moves that will best reflect our new nature. Though the old self is dead, its patterns run deep, and those patterns must be purposefully cast off and forgotten. Over time, as we continue to show up to practice, learn to keep in step with our instructor, and dedicate ourselves to the hard work ahead of us, the righteousness of Christ will become an undeniable mark of our everyday moments.

1. Open today's time with prayer. Thank God for the new nature He's given you through Christ. Ask Him to make your heart's greatest desire to follow Him in obedient worship.

## *Uncover the Original Meaning*

**DECIDE which word you would like to study.**

2. To start your Greek study, look for any potential keywords in Colossians 3:10–17. As you find any repeated word or words

that seem important to the passage, write them in the space provided.

**DISCOVER that word as it was originally written.**

I trust you are getting the hang of looking up the original words. If not, please don't give up! There is so much to be discovered. And, remember, you can always look up words in a regular dictionary for a fuller meaning.

3. Using your preferred tool, discover the original word for *image* in verse 10, and write it below.

***IMAGE =***

**DEFINE that word.**

4. Fill in the chart below for the Greek word you found for *image.*

Greek word: ______________________ Verse and Version: ______________________

| Part of Speech:<br>*(verb, noun, etc.)* | Translation Notes:<br>*(How else is it translated? How often is this word used?)* |
|---|---|
| | |

| Strong's Concordance Number: | Definition: |
|---|---|
| Notes: | |

5. Follow the Greek study steps to look up at least one more word in this week's passage. Here are a few you might start with:

   **renewed (v. 10)**

   **chosen (v. 12)**

   **rule (v. 15)**

If you haven't completed my *Everyday Peace* study (or if you don't remember the meaning of this word), definitely look this one up!

   **dwell (v. 16)**

**Greek word:** ______________________ **Verse and Version:** ______________________

| Part of Speech:<br>*(verb, noun, etc.)* | Translation Notes:<br>*(How else is it translated? How often is this word used?)* |
|---|---|
| Strong's Concordance Number: | Definition: |
| Notes: | |

6. What discoveries did you make through your Clarification study?

You and I were created in the image of God. Every soul on this earth, broken as they are, reveals a bit of who God is. As Christians, we get to be a part of God restoring His image-bearers. Starting from our own attitudes and actions, we get to reflect the character of Christ. With patience and kindness, forgiveness and humility, we are to love the souls around us with the love we ourselves have been bestowed. The way we live out our moments matters. As we purposefully put on the righteous deeds of Christ as our own actions and intentionally follow in the example of Christ with our own attitudes, we reflect an accurate image of Christ to those around us who desperately need to see who He is and how much He loves them. (For more on how we can be image bearers of Christ by loving those around us, check out my *Everyday Love* Bible study on 1 Corinthians 13.)

> {*God, thank You for creating me in Your image. I praise You for Your work in me, the continual newness of the righteousness You've given me through Christ. Help me to walk forward today with purpose to accurately reflect Your glory to those around me.*}

## *Bonus Study*

Follow the Greek study steps for additional words in Colossians 3:10–17 as time allows.

Review your memory work. Consider writing out Colossians 3:10–17 again to help ingrain it into your memory.

# Cheat Sheet

3. Using your preferred tool, discover the original word for *image* in verse 10, and write it below.

   ***IMAGE*** *= εἰκών = EIKŌN*

4. Fill in the chart below for the Greek word you found for *image*.

**Greek word:** *EIKŌN*

**Verse and Version:** *COLOSSIANS 3:10 ESV*

| Part of Speech: *(verb, noun, etc.)* | Translation Notes: *(How else is it translated? How often is this word used?)* |
|---|---|
| noun | image/images (19x), likeness (3x), form (1x) (ESV usage) |
| Strong's Concordance Number: #1504 | Definition: an image, figure, likeness |

Notes:

"Because an image not only implies the likeness of a copy to a model, but derives from an earlier reality, it implies a relation of dependency and of origination; and possessing to some extent the same 'form,' it resembles its precursor." —Ceslas Spicq and James D. Ernest, *Theological Lexicon of the New Testament*

# Utilization

## FOCUSing on Colossians 3:10–17

> *And let us consider how to stir up one another to love and good works, not neglecting to meet together, as is the habit of some, but encouraging one another, and all the more as you see the Day drawing near.*
> *—Hebrews 10:24–25*

**I HATED GROUP** projects in school. I'd rather take on the load by myself and be able to control the outcome. Truth is, I didn't trust anyone to do it as well as I thought I could. People just slowed me down. (I'm a human bulldozer without Jesus.) I have an independent streak that often keeps me from enjoying those around me. I'm simply too busy getting stuff done.

This independence was rudely exposed during my first year of marriage. It often played out like this: I would be in get-it-done mode (truly, I am almost always in get-it-done mode), and Chris would want to engage in playful banter or try to give me a hug and kiss to show his affection for me. I would physically shrug him off and communicate to him as sweetly as I could, "Leave me alone, I'm in the middle of something." I underestimated his need for that physical affection. He underestimated my need to be left alone to do my thing.

When I walked down the aisle, I pledged to do life with Chris, and he with me. We each committed to share and collaborate and learn and grow and exist together. We are part of each other. Early

on in marriage, I think I saw our union as more of a set of railroad tracks on which we chugged forward together—yet separately—toward our goals in life. Instead, we had to learn to become a symbiotic unit—a team.

The commands given in Hebrews 10:24–25 are corporate ones. They definitely have individual implications, but they were not meant for the Christian to practice in isolation. Think about it: every command in this week's passage cannot be carried out alone. They all carry a group connotation—they each require being around other believers in Christ for the individual to carry out. We must be in relationship with people who need compassion, kindness, patience, and forgiveness given to them. (Conversely, we need to surround ourselves with people who will show us that same compassion, patience, and forgiveness.) These commands (and many, many more given in Scripture) are meant for the church.

Even the command in Colossians 3:15–16 to let peace rule and the Word to dwell richly are attached to communal callings. We are called in one body to be at peace. It's not enough to be at peace within while not seeking peace with others. The Word of God needs to dwell within us richly, leading to the teaching and encouraging of one another, the singing together, and thankfulness to God we offer up collectively.

These commands are a group project—a team effort—not a solo endeavor.

1. Ask God to open your eyes to any streaks of independence keeping you from entering into community with other believers. If you are not currently a member of a church, ask God to show you clearly and quickly where He wants you to be. If you are a

part of a church but hanging out on the fringes, ask God to show you where you can serve and with whom you can enter into a deeper relationship. If you are currently in a thriving community of believers, declare your need for Him to love the imperfect souls around you with the love of Christ.

## *Discover the Connections*

2. As a refresher, read Colossians 3:10–17 to start your study.

3. There are so many great cross-references in this passage, it's hard to choose for our time today. Yet, one passage comes up again and again. It is parallel to our passage in many ways. Instead of references to look up for a few phrases, look up and study Ephesians 4:1–6. I think you'll quickly see the many connections between these passages. Study it however you'd like. You could write out all the commands, look up a few Greek words, and/or note how many times the word *one* is used and why you think that might be. You might also note all the truths about the church. Have fun digging!

Many Christians today walk through life without being part of a church. Instead of tethering to a local body of believers, many able-bodied believers settle for listening to a podcast sermon or watching a church service broadcast and calling it "church." Others waste time dating the church, hopping around from place to place, waiting for the perfect church to emerge and for all the warm fuzzies to appear before they finally commit to put down roots. All the while, these believers stay on the outskirts of community, soaking up the service and sacrifice of others without offering up their own time and gifts for the good of those around them.

There is no perfect church. Your pastor and his wife will fail you. The people in the pews will annoy you. You will see sin. You might get hurt. You will probably hurt others. Nonetheless, you need the church and the church needs you. You were built to be in an intertwined relationship with God's people, not on a solitary journey.

If you are a Christian but are perpetually without a church to call home, it's like saying you are in the NBA but not on a team. And if you say you go to a church but show up only when you feel like it and it's convenient for you, that's like saying you are on a team but don't even show up for games, and if you do, it's to sit in the bleachers and watch. It's rather ridiculous, don't you think?

Just so we're clear, I'm not telling you to settle into the very first church you step foot in. It is important to choose a church carefully and prayerfully. Look for a church with these Colossians 3 characteristics: one whose members show the love of Christ to one another and to the community around them; one whose pastor preaches the gospel and accurately handles the Word of truth; one where the peace of Christ rules people's hearts and where the Word of Christ dwells not superficially but richly, resulting in a congregation full of members (not just the pastor) who are teaching and admonishing one another with truth; and one that is filled with worshippers who continually celebrate the glorious grace of our God.

*{Lord, lead us. Stepping into a deeper place with people can be uncomfortable and scary. Show me where I need to be. Give me a heart to be with Your people. Help us to celebrate Your grace in such a way that those who do not know You will be drawn into our midst and pointed to Your glory. Make Your church, Your bride, beautiful, strong, and an accurate picture of one who is wholly in love with You.}*

# *Bonus Study*

Look up cross-references for additional phrases in this week's passage you would like to learn more about.

Continue with your memory work of Colossians 3:10–17. Add your verses to your memory review system.

# Cheat Sheet

3. Look up and study Ephesians 4:1–6.

(There is so much to be seen in this passage! Here are a few truths that stood out to me.)

**Commands**

*walk in a manner worthy of the calling to which you have been called*

*walk with all humility and gentleness, with patience*

*bearing with one another in love*

*be eager to maintain the unity of the Spirit in the bond of peace.*

**Truths about the church**

*there is one body*

*we have one Spirit*

*we are all called to one hope*

*we have one Lord*

*we have one faith*

*we have one baptism*

*we have one God and Father of all*

**Truths about God**

*only one God*

*He is over all and through all and in all*

# Summation

## FOCUSing on Colossians 3:10–17

*Even as he chose us in him before the foundation of the world, that we should be holy and blameless before him . . . according to the purpose of his will, to the praise of his glorious grace. –Ephesians 1:4–6*

**MERE HOURS BEFORE** He was to be betrayed, arrested, and begin His painful pilgrimage to the Cross, Jesus spoke, "I glorified you on earth, having accomplished the work that you gave me to do" *(John 17:4)*. Jesus came to earth out of obedience to the Father, with a desire, above all, to glorify Him. God's glory is what our lives are all about. Our salvation. Our sanctification. Our submission to His ways. That is our purpose in life. It's why Jesus came to earth, and it's why we remain on it. God's glory.

## *Respond to God's Word*

1. Ask God to solidify the change He's begun in you through your time in His Word. Write out a prayer of dedication, committing to God to walk ahead in obedience to all He has shown you through this study.

**IDENTIFY—Find the main idea of the passage.**

2. Take a few moments to flip back to each day's study to review what you've learned this week. In the space provided, write out Colossians 3:10–17 in your own words. Or simply write out what you think the main idea of the passage is, in regard to our study of obedience.

3. Read a commentary or study Bible to see how your observations from this week line up with the scholars. Record any additional observations below.

**MODIFY—Evaluate my beliefs in light of the main idea.**

Prayerfully journal through the following questions, asking the Spirit of God to enlighten and convict you.

4. Do I see obedience as more worship or duty?

5. Do my everyday lifestyle and choices match up with the spiritual reality that I am holy and beloved?

6. What keeps me from truly worshiping with God's people in gospel-centered community?

**GLORIFY—Align my life to reflect the truth of God's Word.**

7. What next step do I need to take to become a more integral part of a local body of believers in Christ?

8. What can I do to move more toward a lifestyle of everyday worship?

9. What is God leading me to work on, in order to sync my everyday living with the internal transformation and calling to bear the image of Christ?

"And whatever you do, in word or deed, do everything in the name of the Lord Jesus, giving thanks to God the Father through him" *(Colossians 3:17)*. Paul sums it all up for us, doesn't He? Whatever you do. Whatever I do. We do it, bearing the name of Jesus, in thankfulness to God.

Everyday obedience: the right response to God's glorious grace.

*{God, I long for my life to be a reflection of You to those around me. Holy Spirit, help me to live a life of everyday obedience, for Your glory.}*

# In Closing

We've come to the end of our study together, and I'm so grateful you've joined me on this journey through Colossians 3:1–17. We've dissected some deep truths together, and I pray that the Holy Spirit has enlightened the eyes of your heart in a transformational, unforgettable way. I hope the excitement and significance of your rescue from a life of sin propels you forward into living a life of worship-filled holiness. More than anything, I trust God has revealed more of who He is and that your view of Him is greater, more vivid, and more majestic than ever before.

Together, lets move forward from our studies and join the ranks of Paul and declare—as he did—the purpose of his holiness, his everyday obedience: "so that in me you may have ample cause to glory in Christ Jesus" *(Philippians 1:26)*.

For His fame,

*Katie*

# Appendix

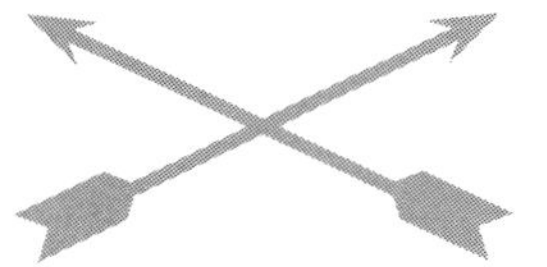

# Truths About Obedience

*Use this space to record all the truths you discover about obedience.*

## Master Sheet

# Glossary of Bible Study Terms

**INTERLINEAR BIBLE:** a translation where each English word is linked to its original Greek word. There are many free interlinear Bibles online, as well as great apps you can download to your phone or tablet. Check out KatieOrr.me/Resources for current links.

**CONCORDANCE:** a helpful list of words found in the original languages of the Bible (mainly Hebrew and Greek) and the verses where you can find them.

**CROSS-REFERENCE:** a notation in a Bible verse that indicates there are other passages that contain similar material.

**FOOTNOTE:** a numerical notation that refers readers to the bottom of a page for additional information.

**COMMENTARY:** a reference book, written by experts, that explains the Bible. A good commentary will give you historical background and language information that may not be obvious from the passage.

**GREEK:** the language in which most of the New Testament was written.

**HEBREW:** the language in which most of the Old Testament was written.

# Structure and Books of the Bible

## *Old Testament*

### Books of the Law (also known as the Pentateuch)

Genesis
Exodus
Leviticus
Numbers
Deuteronomy

### Books of History

Joshua
Judges
Ruth
1 Samuel
2 Samuel
1 Kings
2 Kings
1 Chronicles
2 Chronicles
Ezra
Nehemiah
Esther

### Wisdom Literature

Job
Psalms
Proverbs
Ecclesiastes
Song of Songs

### Major Prophets

Isaiah
Jeremiah
Lamentations
Ezekiel
Daniel

### Minor Prophets

- Hosea
- Joel
- Amos
- Obadiah
- Jonah
- Micah
- Nahum
- Habakkuk
- Zephaniah
- Haggai
- Zechariah
- Malachi

## *New Testament*

### Narratives (First four together are known as the Gospels)

- Matthew
- Mark
- Luke
- John
- Acts

### Epistles (or Letters) by Paul

- Romans
- 1 Corinthians
- 2 Corinthians
- Galatians
- Ephesians
- Philippians
- Colossians
- 1 Thessalonians
- 2 Thessalonians
- 1 Timothy
- 2 Timothy
- Titus
- Philemon

### General Epistles (Letters not by Paul)

- Hebrews
- James
- 1 Peter
- 2 Peter
- 1 John
- 2 John
- 3 John
- Jude

### Apocalyptic Writing

- Revelation

# Major Themes of the Bible

Though many view Scripture as a patchwork of historical accounts, morality tales, and wisdom for daily living, the Bible is really only one story—the mind-blowing story of God's plan to rescue fallen humanity. This storyline flows through every single book, chapter, verse, and word of Scripture. It's crucial that we know the movements, or themes, of the grand storyline so we don't miss the point of the passage we are studying.

For example, I grew up hearing the story of David's adulterous affair with the beautiful but married Bathsheba. I heard how he covered his misdeeds with a murderous plot to snuff out her husband. This story was usually punctuated with a moral that went something like this, "Don't take what isn't yours!" While it is indeed good practice to refrain from taking what isn't ours, there is a much bigger connection to the grand story that we will miss if we stop at a moral lesson. So what then is this grand story, and how can we recognize it?

The story falls into four main themes, or movements: creation, fall, redemption, and completion.*

## *Creation*

The Bible begins by describing the creative work of God. His masterwork and crowning achievement was the creation of people. God put the first couple, Adam and Eve, in absolute paradise and gave them everything they needed to thrive. The best part of this place, the Garden of Eden, was that God walked among His people. They knew Him and were known by Him. The Bible even says they walked around naked because they had no concept of shame or guilt. (See Genesis 2:25.) Life was perfect, just like God had designed.

## *Fall*

In the Garden, God provided everything for Adam and Eve. But He also gave them instructions on how to live and established

boundaries for their protection. Eventually, the first family decided to cross a boundary and break the one rule God commanded them to keep. This decision was the most fateful error in history. At that precise moment, paradise was lost. The connection that people experienced with God vanished. Adam and Eve's act was not simply a mistake but outright rebellion against the sovereign Creator of the universe. It was, in no uncertain terms, a declaration of war against God. Every aspect of creation was fractured in that moment. Because of their choice, Adam and Eve introduced death and disease to the world but more importantly put a chasm between mankind and God that neither Adam nor Eve nor any person could ever hope to cross. Ever since the fall, all people are born with a tendency to sin. Like moths to a light, we are drawn to sin, and like Adam and Eve, our sin pushes us further away from any hope of experiencing God. You see God cannot be good if He doesn't punish sin, but if we all receive the punishment our sin deserves, we would all be cast away from Him forever.

## *Redemption*

Fortunately, God was not caught off guard when Adam and Eve rebelled. God knew they would and had a plan in place to fix what they had broken. This plan meant sending Jesus to earth. Even though Jesus was the rightful King of all creation, He came to earth in perfect humility. He walked the earth for more than 30 years, experiencing everything you and I do. Jesus grew tired at the end of a long day. He got hungry when He didn't eat. He felt the pain of losing loved ones and the disappointment of betrayal from friends. He went through all of life like we do with one massive exception—He never sinned. Jesus never disobeyed God, not even once. Because He was without sin, He was the only one in history who could bridge the gap between God and us. However, redemption came at a steep price. Jesus, the divine Son of God, was nailed to a wooden Cross and left to die a criminal's death. While He hung on the Cross, God put the full weight of our sin upon Jesus. When the King of the universe died, He paid the penalty for our sin. God poured out His righteous anger toward our sin on the sinless One. After Jesus died, He was buried and many believed all hope was lost. However, Jesus did not stay dead—having defeated sin on the Cross, He was raised from death and is alive today!

## *Completion*

The final theme in the grand storyline of the Bible is completion, the end of the story. Now that Jesus has paid the penalty for our sin, we have hope of reconciliation with God. This is such tremendous news because reconciliation means we are forgiven of sin and given eternal life. Reconciliation means God dwells with us again. Finally, we know Him and are known by Him. Completion for us means entering into reconciliation with God through the only means He provided. We can only experience reconciliation under God's rescue plan if we trust Jesus to pay for our sin and demonstrate this by repenting, or turning away, from our sin. But God's rescue plan does not end with us. One day, Jesus will come back and ultimately fix every part of fallen creation. King Jesus will come back to rule over God's people and again establish a paradise free from the effects of sin.

Let's return to the David and Bathsheba story for a moment and try to find our place. David was the greatest, most godly king in the history of the Old Testament, but even he was affected by the Fall and had a sinful nature. This story points out that what we really need is not a more disciplined eye, but a total transformation. We need to be delivered from the effects of the Fall. It also illustrates how we don't simply need a king who loves God, but we need a King who is God. Do you see how this story connects to the arc of the grand storyline? Just look at how much glorious truth we miss out on if we stop short at "don't take what isn't yours."

**For a more detailed discussion on these themes, refer to Part 1 and 2 of* The Explicit Gospel *by Matt Chandler (pages 21–175) or Chapter 2 of Mark Dever's* The Gospel and Personal Evangelism *(pages 31–44).*

# How to Do a Greek/Hebrew Word Study

Learning more about the language used in the original version of Scripture can be a helpful tool toward a better understanding of the author's original meaning and intention in writing. The Old Testament was written in Hebrew and the New Testament in Greek. Though the thought of learning a new language is overwhelming to most of us, we live in an age with incredible tools at our fingertips through smartphone apps and websites (many of which are free!), which make understanding the original meaning as simple as looking a word up in a dictionary.

Here are three easy steps to work toward a better understanding of the verses you study.

**DECIDE which word you would like to study.**

Do a quick read of your passage, and note any potential keywords and/or repeated words. There is no right or wrong way to do this! Simply select a few words you would like to learn more about.

**DISCOVER that word as it was originally written.**

Using an interlinear Bible (see glossary), find the original Greek (if New Testament) or Hebrew (if Old Testament) word for each instance of the word in the passage you are studying. There may be more than one Greek or Hebrew word present that translated into one English word.

**DEFINE that word.**

Look up your Greek or Hebrew word (or words if you found more than one) in a Greek or Hebrew lexicon. Most of the free apps and websites available do this with a simple click of a button, opening up a wealth of information referenced from a lexicon they've chosen. I encourage you to check out the videos I've created to show you how to use many of the online tools. You can find them at KatieOrr.me/Resources.

Though this step can seem overwhelming, once you find an app or site you love, it will become a quick and easy way to dive deeper into the Bible. On the following page, you'll find a chart you can use to record what you learn.

# *Greek/Hebrew Word Study Worksheet*

**Word:** ______________________ **Verse and Version:** ______________________

| Part of Speech:<br>*(verb, noun, etc.)* | Translation Notes:<br>*(How else is it translated? How often is this word used?)* |
|---|---|
| Strong's Concordance Number: | Definition: |
| Notes: | |

# *How to Do a Greek/Hebrew Word Study—Example*

Let's walk through this process looking at Hebrews 11:1 together. I've also included extra notes to help you better understand the behind-the-scenes work the apps and websites are doing for us.

**DECIDE which word you would like to study.**

Since Hebrews is in the New Testament, we'll be working with the Greek language. To start your Greek study, look for any potential keywords in Hebrews 11:1. As you find any repeated word or words that seem important to the passage, write them down.

faith, assurance, hoped, conviction, things, seen

Since faith is probably what the main point of this verse is about, let's study this word together.

**DISCOVER that word as it was originally written.**

Now that we know what we want to study, we can look up the English word faith in an interlinear Bible to find out what the original Greek word is. An interlinear Bible will show you English verses and line up each word next to the Greek words they were translated from. If you own or have seen a parallel Bible, with two or more English translation versions (i.e., ESV, KJV, NIV) lined up next to each other, this is the same concept. Interlinear Bibles have the original language alongside an English translation.

Let's take the first phrase in Hebrews 11:1 to see how this works:

*Now faith is the assurance of things hoped for.*

In Greek, it looks like this: *ἔστιν δὲ πίστις ἐλπιζομένων.*

Most people (including me!) can't read this, so the transliteration of the Greek is often provided for us as well. This transliteration is simply substituting the Greek letter for the corresponding English letters to spell out how the Greek is read.

The interlinear Bible simply lines up the two versions (and typically the transliteration as well), so we can see which word goes with which, like this:

| | | | |
|---|---|---|---|
| *ἔστιν* | *δὲ* | *πίστις* | *ἐλπιζομένων* |
| *estin* | *de* | *pistis* | *elpizomenōn* |
| *is* | *now* | *faith* | *of things hoped for* |

Now you can use this layout to find the original word for *faith*. Do you see it?

*Faith=pistis=πίστις*

**DEFINE that word.**

Now that we know the original word for *faith* used in Hebrews 11:1 is *pistis*, we can look up that Greek word in a Greek lexicon (which is like a dictionary) and note what we learn about the original meaning of the word. I've provided a worksheet to record this info. (For a free printable version of this worksheet, go to KatieOrr.me /Resources and look for the Printables section.)

**Greek word:** *PISTIS*

**Verse and Version:** *HEBREWS 11:1 ESV*

| Part of Speech: *(verb, noun, etc.)* | Translation Notes: *(How else is it translated? How often is this word used?)* |
| --- | --- |
| noun | Used 243 times in the ESV New Testament. All but two times it is translated "faith." Other two translations: assurance (1x) and belief (1x) |
| Strong's Concordance Number: #G4102 | Definition: faith, confidence, fidelity, guarantee, loyalty |

Notes:

"Pistis, which derives from peithomai ('be persuaded, have confidence, obey'), connotes persuasion, conviction, and commitment, and always implies confidence, which is expressed in human relationships as fidelity, trust, assurance, oath, proof, guarantee. Only this richness of meaning can account for the faith (pistei, kata pistin, dia pisteōs) that inspired the conduct of the great Israelite ancestors of Hebrews 11."

# The Good News

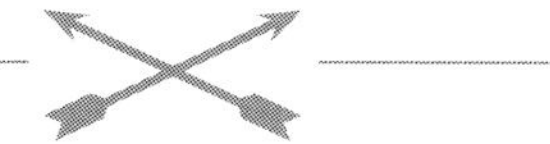

## God Loves You

You are known and deeply loved by a great, glorious, and personal God. This God hand-formed you for a purpose (Ephesians 2:10), He has called you by name (Isaiah 43:1), and you are of great worth to Him (Luke 12:6–7).

## We Have a Sin Problem

We are all sinners and are all therefore separated from God (Romans 3:23; 6:23). Even the "smallest" of sins is a great offense to God. He is a righteous judge who will not be in the presence of sin and cannot allow sin to go unpunished. Our natural tendency toward sin has left us in desperate need of rescue because God must deal with our sin.

## Jesus Is the Only Solution

Since God's standard is perfection, and we have all fallen short of the mark, Jesus is the only answer to our sin problem (John 14:6). Jesus lived a life of perfect obedience to God. So when Jesus died on the Cross, He alone was able to pay the penalty of our sin.

After His death, Jesus rose from the dead, defeating death, and providing the one way we could be reconciled to God (2 Corinthians 5:17–21). Jesus Christ is the only one who can save us from our sins.

## We Must Choose to Believe

Trusting Christ is our only part in the gospel. Specifically, the Bible requires us to have faith in what Christ has done on our behalf (Ephesians 2:8–9). This type of faith is not just belief in God. Many people grow up believing that God exists but never enter into the Christian faith. Faith that saves comes from a desperate heart. A heart that longs for Jesus—the only solution for their sin problem—to be first and foremost in their life. We demonstrate that we have this type of saving faith by turning away, or repenting, from our sin.

# FOCUSed15 Study Method

Apply this method to two to ten verses a day, over a week's time, for a deep encounter with God through His Word, in as little as 15 minutes a day.

## *Foundation: Enjoy Every Word*

Read and rewrite the passage—summarize, draw pictures, diagram sentences, or simply copy the passage. Do whatever helps you slow down and enjoy each word.

## *Observation: Look at the Details*

Take notes on what you see—write down truths in this passage. Look for truths about the character of God, promises to cling to, or commands given.

## *Clarification: Uncover the Original Meaning*

- **Decide which word you would like to study.**
  Look for any repeated words or keywords to look up, choose one, and learn more about it.
- **Discover that word as it was originally written.**
  Using an interlinear Bible, find the original Greek or Hebrew word for the English word you chose.
- **Define that word.**
  Learn the full meaning of the word using a Greek or Hebrew lexicon, which is very much like a dictionary.

## *Utilization: Discover the Connections*

Cross-reference—Look up the references in each verse to view the threads and themes throughout the Bible.

## *Summation: Respond to God's Word*

- **Identify—Find the main idea of the passage.**
- **Modify—Evaluate my beliefs in light of the main idea.**
- **Glorify—Align my life to reflect the truth of God's Word.**

New Hope® Publishers is a division of WMU®, an international organization that challenges Christian believers to understand and be radically involved in God's mission. For more information about WMU, go to wmu.com. More information about New Hope books may be found at **NewHopePublishers.com**. New Hope books may be purchased at your local bookstore.

*If you've been blessed by this book, we would like to hear your story. The publisher and author welcome your comments and suggestions at:*

NEWHOPEREADER@WMU.ORG.

*Use the QR reader on your smartphone to visit us online at* **NewHopePublishers.com**.